Crosscurrents / MODERN CRITIQUES

Harry T. Moore, *General Editor*

Pastoral and Anti-Pastoral Patterns in JOHN UPDIKE'S Fiction

Larry E. Taylor

WITH A PREFACE BY

Harry T. Moore

SOUTHERN ILLINOIS UNIVERSITY PRESS
Carbondale and Edwardsville

FEFFER & SIMONS, INC.
London and Amsterdam

Contents

Preface

Larry E. Taylor's book on John Updike states that Updike is beyond question, "a major American novelist." Mr. Taylor's critique of that writer's fiction convincingly deals with the important themes of the novels and short stories seen principally in terms of the pastoral, whether pro-, mock-, or anti-. Mr. Taylor's exposition and analysis are expert and masterful. They begin with Updike's earliest work and bring us up to date with a thorough discussion of Bech: A Book.

Mr. Taylor provides an interesting (and mercifully brief) history of the pastoral, from the times when Theocritus usually composed his rural-worshipping Idylls with the hills around Arcady or memories of them in the background, and Mr. Taylor also discusses Virgil's Georgics and Eclogues, so full of the countryside near Mantua. Mr. Taylor then examines American literature from its beginnings and shows us how various forms of the pastoral have been present from the first. He usefully gives special attention to Thoreau and to Walden, commenting on its use of different phases of the pastoral.

Some more recent authors are also mentioned, however briefly, including Ernest Hemingway, who wrote with such forceful nostalgia about the rivers and forests of his childhood experiences in northern Michigan, and Willa Cather, whose novels and stories so often re-created the Nebraska plains of her youth. As for Sinclair Lewis, we are shown how the apparently pastoral elements in Babbitt turn toward the anti-pastoral mode.

Mr. Taylor also shows how skillfully John Updike uses both these modes, so that no further direct commentary is needed here. But I want to reinforce one of Mr. Taylor's points, namely that Updike is in the mainstream of American tradition. Mr. Taylor discusses him in terms of his fellow writers of major stature; I want to mention two minor novels which are forerunners of his book, The Centaur, as well as point out a parallel with one element of Scott Fitzgerald's The Great Gatsby.

John Updike and Larry Taylor are too young to know very much about the excitement that raged around Cyril Hume's novel Wife of the Centaur in 1923 and for a few years after (M.G.M. made it into a film with John Gilbert, Eleanor Boardman, and Aileen Pringle). Hume's book was somewhat in the Fitzgerald vein—he was twenty-three when the novel came out—and it dealt with the life of a poet. Jeff Dwyer was shown at prep school, at Yale, in the army, and then as a beginning novelist. Many of his actions were paralleled in long italicized passages presenting the centaur in his wild youth and later as a somewhat older figure being tamed by Pallas Athena ("as in that dark old picture by Botticelli").

Hume for a while had a Fitzgerald-like youthful fame which dissolved after his second novel, Cruel Fellowship, a better book, in my allowance, than Wife of the Centaur. He became a more successful screen writer than Fitzgerald, though his talent was largely wasted when he wrote the scenario and dialogue of a series of Tarzan films. (I met him in Hollywood and told him I'd heard Thornton Wilder say that Fitzgerald would pick up a volume of Flaubert and groan, "Once I thought I'd someday be able to write prose like that"—and then he'd go out to be sick. Hume, who looked like Teddy Roosevelt, grinned toothily and said, "Oh, that's just Scott's way of dramatizing himself.")

Fitzgerald's biographer, Arthur Mizener, in an essay ("The American Novel and Nature in the Twentieth Century") in his book, The Sense of Life in the Modern Novel, speaks of Hume's Wife of the Centaur as one of the popular novels of the early 1920s which provide the most intimate depiction of the life of that time, "a revelation." And, surely, to some of us who were then in high school (as Arthur Mizener and I were—both in Pennsylvania), Jeff Dwyer became, centaur and all, a persona we frequently used before we discovered Stephen Dedalus and, much later, Dick Diver.

The last two have become a standard part of the literature of English-speaking people; but Jeff Dwyer didn't survive the 1920s except as a faint memory to those who once, partially at least, had identified with him.

Cyril Hume became a successful television writer and died a few years ago. His Wife of the Centaur may never be reprinted. I've several times tried to get it republished, but have failed. Yet the centaur stamps on, even though Messrs. Updike and Taylor probably never heard of Hume's version of the matter.

There is still another centaur novel of the 1920s: Murray Sheehan's Half-Gods (1927), which apparently takes its title from Emerson's

> When half-gods go
> The gods arrive.

In Sheehan's story, a centaur is born on a Missouri farm. The Durnans, the family which owns the farm, are at first ashamed, but eventually they make use of the creature by renting him to a carnival; and a professor of Classics from the nearby university is delighted because he can converse in Greek with the centaur, whose "double" is the sensitive young Daniel Durnan. Daniel leaves at the end, like George Willard in Anderson's Winesburg, Ohio, but the centaur eventually yields to the mediocre standards of the community and, after displaying some human foibles, realizes his most intense ambition by becoming "one of the fellows at the corner store."

Half-Gods didn't have anything like the success of Wife of the Centaur, perhaps because it was written in a flat prose while Hume's book had at least a tricky style. In any event, Sheehan provided another possible ancestor of Updike's centaur, though once again it is probable that neither John Updike nor Larry Taylor has ever heard of Half-Gods. I've mentioned these books only because they provide a marginal note to the present volume, whose author discusses the pastoral and anti-pastoral tradition solely in terms of truly major (Faulkner) or of consistently popular (Steinbeck) writers. For, in addition to the general pastoral, mock-pastoral, and anti-pastoral mode in American literature, there is also, however minor, a centaur tradition.

Maybe someone has already pointed this out. I don't know all the literature on Updike, but at least I've given the subject a certain slant here.

There is one more point about this author that shows how firmly he is rooted in the tradition. "Rabbit" Angstrom of Rabbit, Run has at least one thing in common with Tom Buchanan in Fitzgerald's The Great Gatsby: their early successes as athletes have made their later lives anticlimactic. They are far different in social status, and Tom can buy himself a new polo-pony whenever he wishes to console himself —but there is a resemblance in that both feel lost after their respective basketball and football days are over. We can hardly say that John Updike didn't know The Great Gatsby, but he may not have been consciously aware that he was using a Fitzgerald theme. Of course Fitzgerald applied it only to a secondary character, and the idea of the superannuated is an old one indeed in literature; and often in primitive societies the killing or dethroning of elders was a built-in custom. However that may be, John Updike made Angstrom a character in his own right, and his relation to pastoral and anti-pastoral ideas is skillfully presented by Larry E. Taylor, as everything in this book is. And now the reader can see all this for himself.

HARRY T. MOORE

Southern Illinois University
September 21, 1970

Introduction

The theme of this book is that a strong current of the pastoral and anti-pastoral tradition and mode runs through the history of American fiction, that the tradition has not received adequate critical attention, and that the pattern has become increasingly important in the past three or four decades. Further, variations of the pastoral motif (and the inescapably concomitant anti-pastoral or mock-pastoral) have become outstanding formal and thematic modes of expression for several of the most important and sophisticated artists of our time. Among these more recent users are Saul Bellow, Ken Kesey, Flannery O'Connor, Carson McCullers, Eudora Welty, Truman Capote, Bernard Malamud, John Barth, and, most prominently, John Updike. In this book I shall attempt to define, clarify, and examine in detail this pastoral mode as it is employed in the fiction of John Updike, the subtlest and, at the same time, the most obvious user of pastoral and anti-pastoral techniques. Thus, my aim is twofold: 1) to examine a tradition, and 2) to show how that tradition works in the body of a particular author's art.

My first aim, to trace a tradition, is the more difficult task, a little like the archaeologist's job of sifting through geological strata where one city has been built upon the ruins of another over centuries. After all, I will be using terminology ("the pastoral") which was originally used to describe literature which flourished in the third century B.C. Fortunately, both the reader and I will be invaluably assisted by two important works in making the epic leap from Theocritus (c. 360 B.C.) to *The Centaur* (1963), to *Of the Farm* (1965), to *Couples* (1968). The books are *Some Versions of Pastoral*, by William Empson (London, 1935), and *The Pastoral Art of Robert Frost*, by John F. Lynen (New Haven, 1960). Both works essentially support my basic thesis about the pastoral and anti-pastoral modes. Empson's book, sociologically and psychologically oriented, asserts the existence of the pattern in British literature from the Renaissance to the latter part of the nineteenth century—from Shakespeare through Fielding to Lewis Carroll. Lynen's aesthetically oriented work provides an excellent general delineation of the pattern in American literature, and his application of his thesis to Robert Frost's poetry is indispensable for reading Frost. However, neither book deals with American prose fiction; to my knowledge, no thorough treatment of the pastoral pattern exists in this particular area. I hope, by this essay, to help fill this important gap.

Admittedly, in choosing the term *pastoral* to describe the patterns rather than, say, "agrarian," "return to nature," "transcendental," "rural," or "bucolic," I am placing myself outside the main stream of most recent criticism of American prose fiction. But I choose the term deliberately. And, to avoid being labeled what C. S. Lewis calls a "style-monger" (a critic who sees literature as nothing more than a series of pleasing styles and forms), I shall treat the pastoral and anti-pastoral not merely as a literary technique, but also as a significant theme. By significant, I mean that the pastoral in the American tradition both *means* and *is*; it encompasses both a theme and a technique, a subject and an attitude toward the subject; it has psychological validity, as well as sociological and historical substance. At times, the pastoral and anti-pastoral are, to be sure, mere conventions; at times, they are myths; almost always the patterns are metaphors.

In tracing the tradition and as a way of introducing my topic, I first examine the broad literary areas where the terms "pastoral" and "anti-pastoral" apply; here I define my terms primarily through descriptions of well-known works. Second, I trace the pattern as it has developed in America up to the present time. Third, I show how the tradition relates to John Updike's fiction.

LARRY E. TAYLOR

Carbondale, Illinois
15 August 1970

Pastoral and Anti-Pastoral Patterns
in John Updike's Fiction

1

The Pastoral and Anti-Pastoral Modes

Let us start at the beginning. Theocritus, the third century B.C. Greek poet, originated the pastoral form and manner. Although pastoralism has meant different things to different artists in the centuries since Theocritus, the mode has existed in either the serious or the ironic (mock) form down to the present time. When John Updike writes a short story about jet-set adultery in a February 1968, edition of the *New Yorker* and includes two lengthy, italicized, formally isolated, idyllically phrased lover's laments, the reader is forced to recall similar tones and images from pastoral idyls:

Oh Sally, my lost only Sally, let me say now, now before we both forget, while the spark still lives on the waterfall, that I love you, that the sight of you shamed my eyes. You were a territory where I went on tiptoe to steal a magic mirror, a hyperbolic image of my worth. I would go to meet you as a knight, to rescue you, and would become instead the dragon, and ravish you. You weighed me out in jewels, though ashes were what I could afford.[1]

. . . .

Oh Sally, it was such a beautiful ride! Do you remember at what a low altitude we flew? How our little plane, like a swan boat mildly bobbing in an occasional current, carried us through the middle air that was spangled with constellations above and cities below? I saw, past the halo of your sleeping hair, the capital's continent of light expand, tilt, and expand again: Dante could not have dreamed such a rose. Our DC–3, fetched from Heaven knows where to carry us home, was chilly—unheated, unpressurized; it was honest ether we inhaled.[2]

Furthermore, while the adulterous couple in Updike's story take a respite from the harrowing ordeal of trying to get plane tickets during an airlines strike, they find a tiny cool patch of grass outside the terminal, where they ironically and mockingly dream the pastoral dream:

Her toes felt cool out of her shoes, and her man regained his reality in the presence of air and grass.

"I see us," he said, stretching his arm toward the distance, "in Wyoming, with your children, and a horse, and a cold little lake we can swim in, and a garden we can make near the house." [3]

That apostrophic and lyrical "Oh Sally, my lost only Sally" is an echo of "Ah, lovely Amaryllis, why no more, as of old, dost thou glance through this cavern after me, nor callest me, thy sweetheart, to thy side." [4] Those "sparks on the waterfall," that "swan boat mildly bobbing," that "spangled middle air," that "halo of your sleeping hair," that "honest ether," are all ironic linguistic echoes of nothing short of the pastoral lover's lament, joined here in the lover's mind with echoes of medieval dragons, knights, and jewels. That horse and garden and cold little lake in Wyoming are ironic linguistic and imagistic signposts pointing the reader back through the centuries to the springs and goats and gardens and horses of the Theocritan idyl.

But the idyllic apostrophes and the pastoral dream of Wyoming are made striking and significant in the story because of their dramatic contrast to the pressure of the airport, the DC–3, the Hertz credit cards, the totally nonpastoral setting and society. The adultery itself—messy, neurotic, tawdry as it is—contrasts to the freshness and simplicity of Corydon and Amaryllis' ideal love relationship. The effect of irony relies on the technique of anti-pastoral as surely as Shakespeare's *As You Like It* relies on anti-pastoral.

My point is that in the 1960s the stories within the covers of the *New Yorker*, for instance, contain elements of the pastoral tradition as obvious as, say, those covers themselves. Those cover pictures are, in fact, quite pertinent to the general topic of pastoralism in the twentieth century.

With predictable regularity they display simply drawn, stylized scenes of fields of daisies and sunflowers, gardens of radishes and corn, window boxes of begonias, rustic New England seaports, glowing autumnal trees, bucolic snow scenes—all blatantly pastoral, and all the antithesis of the other favorite cover theme—city shops, apartments, metropolitan sophistication. As John Updike himself has wryly said of his own first person plural writings for "The Talk of the Town" sections of the *New Yorker*, "Who, after all, could that indefatigably fascinated, perpetually peripatetic 'we' be but a collection of dazzled farmboys?" [5]

It is no accident that America's most sophisticated magazine, the *New Yorker*, contains the most important examples of pastoral art. From Theocritus to Robert Frost (in poetry), to John Updike (in prose), to Andrew Wyeth (in painting), the pastoral mode, for all its studied and stylized "simplicity," remains a technique for highly sophisticated artists. For example, take Theocritus himself as the prototype for the serious pastoral artist, and compare him to other writers who have employed the theme and technique in its *serious* form. (Notice that I make a clear distinction between serious pastoral and mock pastoral—a distinction that becomes increasingly important in American literature, as I shall later indicate.)

This sophistication of the original Theocritan and Virgilian pastoral mode is familiar to students of classical Greek and Roman literature, as it is familiar to students of Milton, Pope, and Frost. John Addington Symonds, the Victorian neoclassicist, associates the Greek poet with the sophisticated and artificial Alexandrian court:

> Theocritus flourished between 283 and 263 B.C., but the dates and circumstances of his birth and death are alike unknown. We may gather, inferentially or directly from his poems, that he sought the patronage of Ptolemy Philadelphus at Alexandria, and lived for some time among the men of letters at his court. Indeed, Theocritus was the most brilliant ornament of that somewhat artificial period of literature.[6]

Thus, the original pastoral artist was a man alienated from his subject matter, a man looking back to a simpler bucolic life, a life idealized and stylized because of its distance in time and space.

In establishing the sophistication of the pastoral mode, William Empson (who rightly led the way in modern criticism toward seeing the pastoral as much more than a mere convention) distinguishes between "proletarian literature" and pastoral. He says: "But most fairy stories and ballads, though 'by' and 'for,' are not 'about' simple, rural subjects; whereas pastoral though 'about' is not 'by' or 'for.' " [7] Furthermore, Empson continues

> The essential trick of the old pastoral, which was felt to imply a beautiful relation between rich and poor, was to make a simple people express strong feelings (felt as the most universal subject, something fundamentally true about everybody) in learned and fashionable language (so that you wrote about the best subject in the best way). From seeing the two sorts of people combined like this you thought better of both; the best parts of both were used. The effect was in some degree to combine in the reader or author the merits of the two sorts; he was made to mirror in himself more completely the effective elements of the society he lived in. This was not a process that you could explain in the course of writing pastoral; it was already shown by the clash between style and theme, and to make the clash work in the right way (not become funny) the writer must keep up a firm pretence that he was unconscious of it.[8]

Empson is pushing a sociological thesis about the pastoral, of course, but his comments are sound. Consider the extent to which *Lycidas, Walden, The Centaur,* and John Barth's *Giles Goat-Boy* are either "by" or "for" simple, uneducated rural people. Footnotes, glossaries, commentaries, and explications are necessary for the understanding of all these highly sophisticated works. The rusticity of Thoreau's cabin, the simplicity of Updike's Caldwell-Centaur, the commonness of Frost's birches and snows are all about as unsophisticated as Harvard University itself, where these three major American pastoral artists were educated. Likewise, Theocritus' pastorals are about as unsophisticated as the urbane Alexandrian Court.

Thus far, I have approached the definition of the serious pastoral mode by discussing the viewpoint and attitude of the author, an author who will generally conform to the prototype of Theocritus. Two conclusions can be drawn about this attitude and authorial position: 1) either intellectually or environmentally, the author will have experienced alienation from the innocent, simple, "natural," rural existence found in the setting and subject of the pastoral; and 2) he will celebrate, idealize, and mythologize (in the Jungian psychological sense,[9] if not in the formal literary sense) that lost innocence, simplicity, and naturalness.

John F. Lynen, in defining the pastoral mode as it relates to Robert Frost, agrees that the pattern is essentially a matter of authorial point of view:

The pastoral genre can best be defined as a particular synthesis of attitudes toward the rural world. One might call this a point of view. It is one not to be found in every age, and among poets, at least, it is rare today. However, pastoral has had its periods of vigorous growth—notably during the cultural ascendancy of Alexandria, the age of Virgil, and the Renaissance. We need not seek for elaborate social explanations. Pastoral comes to life whenever the poet is able to adopt its special point of view—whenever he casts himself in the role of the country dweller and writes about life in terms of the contrast between the rural world, with its rustic scenery and naive, humble folk, and the great outer world of the powerful, the wealthy, and the sophisticated. Though rural life is the subject of pastoral, it is not seen in and for itself: the poet always tends to view it with reference to the more sophisticated plane of experience upon which both he and his audience live.[10]

The pastoral tradition implies a conflict between the sophisticated world the author (or character in prose fiction) finds himself in, and the "natural," unsophisticated world he longs for. Thus, we see an essentially dramatic situation—the kind of conflict necessary for such basic tensions as those found in *Walden*, where Thoreau is pulled from the pencil factory and literary salon to the banks of Walden; where Mark Twain writes longingly and sometimes idyllically of *Life on the Mississippi*, and where Huck Finn is pulled from the corrupt towns to the simple raft life; where George F. Babbitt longs for the fairy child and the Maine Woods; where Jake Barnes and Bill Gorton escape the senseless drinking and sex bouts to catch trout and drink spring-cooled wine; where West's Miss Lonelyhearts spends an idyllic weekend in the country; where Updike's Rabbit Angstrom becomes a gardener and finally runs off into the woods; where jet-set adultery is juxtaposed against an idyllic love lyric and a pastoral dream of Wyoming. Thus, alienation and loss of traditional beliefs and values are stimuli for pastoral literature. It seems significant, then, that Hesiod, the ninth-century B.C. Greek writer, was a poor farmer who lived a hard, bitter life, and wrote *Works and Days* and the *Theogony*, an "account of the creation of the universe and the generation of the gods." [11] Theocritus, on the other hand, was a sophisticated member of the intellectual, urbane, corrupt third-century B.C. Alexandrian Court, and wrote pastorals.

Having established that an important part of the pastoral mode is the author's (or fictional character's) attitude toward a particular subject, I shall now examine that subject itself in more depth. In the serious pastoral tradition, it is safe to say that the subject is 1) people of a low socio-economic class, 2) living in simplicity and harmony, 3) against a background of rural nature. In the classical pattern, this subject emerges as 1) Corydon, Lycidas, and Amaryllis, 2) tending their flocks, weaving garlands, and singing songs, 3) out among the fields, caves, and brooks of Arcady. In the Christian-Judaic pattern, it is Adam and Eve spinning and gardening in Eden. (It may also be John the Baptist eating locusts and wild honey in the wilderness, or Jesus, the shepherd, exhorting his flock to "Consider the lilies of the field" on the banks of Galilee.)

The proliferation of the pastoral convention in the Renaissance has been the subject of several good scholarly works.[12] Sidney's *Arcadia*, Lodge's *Rosalynde*, Spenser's *Shepheardes Calendar* provide good examples of serious pastoralism. It is significant, however, that by the time of the Renaissance, pastoralism must often be talked about in terms of *elements;* that is, the *Arcadia, Rosalynde,* and *The Faerie Queene* are said to contain clearly discernible *elements of pastoralism* (along with elements of romance or epic, for example), much in the same way that modern American fiction contains elements of pastoralism (along with elements of realism or naturalism, for example.) The significance of these elements is that, thematically and formally, the tradition has descended even to modern times as a convention or mode—often a kind of stylistic mannerism, and almost always a thematic touchstone. Thus, in the modern American novel, a "realistic" novel will often contain at least one chapter which is clearly pastoral (for example, as in the chapter "Miss Lonelyhearts in the Country" in Nathanael West's *Miss Lonelyhearts,* the trout-fishing chapter in Hemingway's *The Sun Also Rises,* or Babbitt's flight to the Maine Woods in *Babbitt*). In Updike's *The Centaur* (which may be seen as a kind of pastoral elegy), much of the power of the novel depends on the tensions resulting from the thematic and formal shifts from realism to pastoralism to epic. *Of the Farm* is a type of pastoral idyl. Updike's novel *Couples* totters between pastoral and anti-pastoral; as Updike has said of *Couples,* "All these goings-on would be purely lyrical, like nymphs and satyrs in a grove, except for the group of distressed and neglected children." [13]

As William Empson points out in his analysis of pastoralism, the mode is implicitly moral to the extent that it shows simple, lower-class, rural life as being better than complex, upper-class, urban life.[14] The a priori assumption of the serious pastoral is that something inherently good exists in the simple rural life, and something inherently bad exists in the sophisticated urban life.[15] As I will demonstrate below, the challenge to this a priori generalization becomes the basis for the *anti*-pastoral tradition. Critics of American literature have readily perceived that this basic moral assumption about rural simplicity exists as a main current in American literature and thought; but, for some reason, the critics have largely failed to see the assumption in terms of the prototype, classical pastoralism and anti-pastoralism.[16]

To further analyze the subject matter of the pastoral tradition, I must consider another part of William Empson's theory. He suggests that in the English versions of the pastoral *attitude* (from the Renaissance even to the present) it is not uncommon for the artist to lose sight of the original prerequisite of a bucolic, rural setting; subsequently, the writer may tend to treat *any* lower socioeconomic class with the attitude originally reserved for shepherds and simple cultivators of the soil.[17] Thus, Empson explains such phenomena as the double plots of Renaissance drama; the *Beggar's Opera*; the child cult of Wordsworthian romanticism; the clarity of Alice's vision in the corrupt, distorted "Wonderland"; and the Dickensian cast of poor-but-noble children, blacksmiths, housekeepers, convicts, and London slum-dwellers. By extension, Empson's theory could be used to explain the tendency of English and American novels to concentrate on heroes and heroines like Moll Flanders, Tom Jones, David Copperfield, Pip, Ishmael, Huck Finn, Maggie, Sister Carrie, et cetera—from Natty Bumppo and Horatio Alger's heroes, down to Faulkner's Joe Christmas, and Updike's Caldwell-Centaur. The implication is that the point of view inherent in the pastoral mode itself, with its emphasis on a proletarian or lower-class subject, is not nearly so far removed from contemporary egalitarian and democratic viewpoints as might first be supposed.

To support and explain his theory, Empson cites the double plots of Renaissance drama, in which the subplot often centered on a pastoral or, at least, proletarian subject. For example, he cites the "Falstaff plot" of *Henry IV*, the "Wagner plot" of *Dr. Faustus*, and the whole tradition of "mixing kings and clowns." Almost always in Renaissance and Jacobean drama, these proletarians or lower-class characters act as foils or contrasts to the "nobler" (i.e., better educated, wealthier, more sophisticated) characters. Although I cannot entirely agree with Empson's theory about the double plots, the technique does, beyond a doubt, remind one of the *attitude* behind the Theocritan pastoral, to the extent that the humble shepherds of the Idyls are implicitly contrasted to the unattractive sophistication of the Alexandrian court. (If we do accept this parallel, the Falstaffian plot becomes an example of an *anti-pastoral* attitude rather than a serious pastoral attitude.) Certainly, Empson's theory is fascinating, if not totally convincing.

While agreeing that a pastoral attitude may essentially underlie an author's treatment of lower-class subjects (whether those subjects be poor urban characters or poor rural characters), I am not prepared to abandon the requisite inclusion of some treatment of a rural, or bucolic, or agrarian, or natural subject matter somewhere within the pastoral and anti-pastoral pattern. It can be the Compson family's golf course, the Caldwell farm, or "The Green" of Tarbox, Massachusetts, but it must have some grass or trees. Insofar as elements of the pastoral and anti-pastoral traditions exist in twentieth-century American fiction, they exist in some relation to a "return to nature" motif, or a "nature myth," or an "agrarian mystique." Thus, while it is rewarding and necessary to talk about pastoral and anti-pastoral patterns in the work of Frost, Hemingway, Faulkner, Cather, Welty, Flannery O'Connor, James Agee, Steinbeck, Bellow, John Barth, and especially John Updike, it is a little preposterous and pedantic to extend pastoralism to include *any* lower-class subject (like James Baldwin's characters in *Another Country*)—that is, to extend the pattern to the lengths included in Empson's theory. Thus, not merely an attitude toward a social class, but a specific *attitude toward nature* must exist before a work can rightly be discussed in terms of the pastoral tradition.

This matter of nature is one of the most important parts of the pastoral tradition in American literature. Pastoralism treats nature in a distinctive way—whether in Theocritus' *Idyls*, Thoreau's *Walden*, or John Updike's *Rabbit, Run* or *Of the Farm*. Perhaps the best way to approach the topic is to make a distinction between "nature writing" and "pastoralism." John F. Lynen makes such a distinction in his discussion of *The Pastoral Art of Robert Frost*:

Frost's nature poetry is so excellent and so characteristic that it must be given a prominent place in any account of his art. In our attempt to understand this aspect of Frost, the idea of pastoral proves useful. Not that the nature poems are to be considered as pastorals in any strict sense—obviously the two kinds of poetry differ. In pastorals the subject is a special society, or, more generally, a way of life, and nature is merely the setting within which we see this. The pastoralist does not write *about* nature; he uses nature as his scene, and it is important only in that it defines the swain's point of view. Nevertheless, Frost's nature poetry is closely related to his pastoralism.[18]

The important distinction here is that pastoralism concentrates on "a special society" or a "way of life," rather than on the trees and lakes and rocks themselves. Thus, *Walden*, for example, is not about the ponds and woods, but about the way Thoreau *exists* in the woods, and about what he *sees* in the woods; it is about Thoreau himself. Similarly, when John Updike creates characters (like the mothers in "Pigeon Feathers," *The Centaur*, and *Of the Farm*) who passionately cling to the land and to theories of "organic farming," he is not merely dealing with a "return to nature" theme, but with a way of life, and an entire myth and tradition about that way of life. If an artist shows that life and myth to be lost, absurd, untenable, or false (as Shakespeare does in *As You Like It*, or Sinclair Lewis does in *Babbitt*), then he works in the tradition of anti-pastoral.

In addition, the pastoral and anti-pastoral modes will always deal with myth and metaphor. Since it is now fashionable for literary ctitics to argue long and loud and tiresomely about the definition of "myth," let me be unmodishly brief and concise. First, "myth" can mean widely known fables, legends, or stories originally produced to explain in concrete and symbolic images certain natural, psychological, and spiritual phenomena. In this sense, the story of a man named Sisyphus, who is assigned the unending task of rolling a stone up a mountain, is a myth. Thus, myth is what is meant when we speak of Greek, Hebraic, Christian, Scandinavian, or Oriental "mythology."

Second, "myth" can mean certain vague, unformulated mystiques, codes, and beliefs current and viable in a large segment of a given society at a given time; these are what C. G. Jung would call "myths of the collective unconscious." [19] Linguistically, we refer to these myths when we talk about "the southern myth of racial superiority," or "the agrarian myth," or "the new England myth," or "the pastoral myth," or "the myth of the All-American hero." Third, myth can mean any highly personal story, legend, fable, mystique, or code which a given individual creates in order to help explain and structure his or another person's particular life. Thus, we could say that Ernest Hemingway created the "myth of the athlete and the stiff upper lip," or that one's uncle has a "myth about Fords." To my way of seeing, these three senses include all the semantic possibilities of the word.

From this explanation, it should be clear to the reader that when I say John Updike makes use of the "Centaur myth" I mean myth in the sense of Greek mythology. When I say he employs the "pastoral myth," I mean the formal, thematic, and moral implications of both an attitude and a subject matter which can be traced back to the prototypic Theocritan pastoral—the whole body of pastoral assumptions as I have dealt with them in this chapter. When I refer to the "American agrarian myth," I mean a generalized American attitude toward nature, the land, and rural life—an attitude historically traceable and still current in large segments of American culture.

This introduction of myth into the discussion of the pastoral and anti-pastoral modes demands further consideration, especially in connection with heroic traditions. One of the major concerns in twentieth-century fiction has been the problem of heroes and "anti-heroes." [20] In the case of James Joyce and John Updike, two twentieth-century novelists have created novels with titles directly linking their heroes to classical heroic Greek mythology—*Ulysses* and *The Centaur*. The novels have more than titular links with myth and with each other; in several ways, the two novels reflect a deep, pervasive understanding of the classical Greek concept of metaphor—an understanding comparable to, say, John Milton's understanding of classical Greek myth and metaphor. And as Milton employed classical forms, traditions, and myths to deal with the most vital themes of his life and time (he includes an attack on the corrupt clergy in the pastoral *Lycidas,* and his own blindness is in the background of the tragic *Samson Agonistes*), both Joyce and Updike employ these traditions and myths to deal with their (and our) most important contemporary issues. On one level, one can explain this use of myths as a kind of artistic pragmatism; that is, the story of Ulysses and the story of the Centaur are conveniences in that the two myths have an archetypal correspondence to themes and situations which Joyce and Updike find important in their own times, or any time, or *all* time, for that matter.

But everyone will agree that there is much more to the use of myth in *Ulysses* and *The Centaur* than the mere application of old mythologies to new settings—a kind of cultural exchange program between ancient Greece and modern Ireland and Pennsylvania! Perhaps the best way of understanding a large part of what both Joyce and Updike are doing is to understand the link between epic (the "highest" literary genre, according to the pigeon-holing critics of the eighteenth-century's "theory of genre") and pastoral (the"lowest" genre, according to the same theory). Both Joyce and Updike chose heroes who are distinguished, singled out, and made conspicuous by their very ordinariness—their pedestrian, frustration-fraught, lower-middle-class, anxious little lives. But Bloom and Caldwell are the best possible heroes of our time—they manage to survive, and they manage to love. This attitude and choice of subject—this singling out of a high-school science teacher as the hero (the Centaur) who saves the hero (Prometheus) —has pastoral implications in itself, even if Updike had not included the rural-urban motif and all the other pastoral elements in the novel.

The link between the "pastoral hero" (the simple, unheroic swain) and the "epic hero" (the cunning, sophisticated saviour) is a subtle one. The link rests on three assumptions of the pastoral mode: 1) The simple, rural, lower-class shepherd is closer to elemental nature in his life and vision; 2) because his way of life is more elemental and more harmonious with universal nature than the life of the alienated sophisticate, then his way of life is *better* than the sophisticate's; 3) hence, being *better*, it is closer to the old heroic age—to the hero who is the *best* of all mankind. The pastoral points to the Promethean and Adamic hero—to a time before the Fall, to a pre-lapsarian idyl. If the pastoral life is not always pleasant, and nature is not always benevolent, still the very conflict with nature is an elemental, vital conflict.

This paradoxical connection between the pastoral and heroic is discussed by William Empson. He views the question in relation to "Homer as the fountainhead of simplicity":

. . . the fact seems to be that both [heroic and pastoral] rely on a "complex in simple" formula.

One idea essential to a primitive epic style is that the good is not separable (anyway at first level judgments) from a life of straightforward worldly success in which you keep certain rules; the plain satisfactions are good in themselves and make great the men who enjoy them. From this comes the "sense of glory" and of controlling nature by delight in it. . . . The naive view is so often more true than the sophisticated ones that this comes in later ages to take on an air of massive grandeur; it gives a feeling of freedom from humbug which is undoubtedly noble, and the Homeric heroes support this by the far from savage trait of questioning the beliefs they still die for. . . . it is assumed that Ajax is still enormously grand when he cooks his dinner; the later reader feels he must really be very grand not to lose his dignity, whereas at the time it was a thing of some splendour to have so much dinner to cook or such implements to do it with. This comes to have the same effect as a pretence of pastoral humility in the author. Also the heroic individual has an enormous effect on everything in sight, gods, and men, and yet finds everything of manageable dimensions; the later reader feels that this belongs to a village society rather than a large-town one.[21]

Thus, in twentieth-century fiction, the writer links Ulysses and Leopold Bloom; or Chiron and George Caldwell; Christ and Joe Christmas; Pan and Giles Goat-Boy. And the attitude and technique are similar to that of the original Theocritan pastoral mode, where the simple shepherd Lycidas is linked in the reader's mind to Pan himself, or to the pattern in which gods and heroes are often assigned the humblest tasks (Apollo as the slave and servant of Admetus, or Hercules as a stable cleaner). Apollo, attending Admetus' sheep on the hillside, is no less a god; Hercules, cleansing a stable, is no less a hero. Indeed, classical heroic literature as a whole is often based on the most basic and frustrating and petty parts of life—concern for marital fidelity, the production of adequate food, curing of illness, spinning, weaving, eating, drinking—all those earthy phenomena which fill men's lives. If one wants to read about "the phrase and carriage of everyday life," one might do better to read Homer than William Dean Howells and the daily newspaper! The general failure of Howellsian "realism" in the twentieth century may owe as much to a sophisticated new understanding of heroic myth and metaphor as it owes to the inherent dull limits of W. D. Howells' theory itself. The curious mixture of photographic "real grasshoppers" (W. D. Howells' term) and "specificity of detail" (Henry James's term) along with classical mythology that we find in the work of, for example, James Joyce and John Updike should be related to the heroic, pastoral, and anti-pastoral modes. Updike's fiction is at times painfully burdened with "specificity of detail" in his *New Yorker* passion for brand names, labels, "close-ups," minutiae, and trivia. At times we may feel that the modern equivalent of epic "catalogues" of armors, warriors, and ships is the modern fiction writer's "catalogue" of brand names and routine trivia. Perhaps this is merely another sign of linkage between pastoral, epic, and realism: the epic writer has his catalogue; the pastoral writer has his lists of flowers and herbs; the realist has his brand names and exaggerated cinematic close-ups.

The relation between the heroic and the pastoral genres is perhaps nowhere better illustrated than in Henry David

Thoreau's *Walden*. Indeed, in the American tradition, *Walden* may provide one of the best examples of a pastoral mode and a pastoral hero (and perhaps even an example of the prototypic American antihero). *Walden* is couched in terms of a heroic quest—from details such as Thoreau's daily reading matter (Greek heroic literature) to his constant allusions to myth and poetry and heroism; at the same time, Thoreau concentrates on the homeliest, most essential elements of his way of life. Consider his emphasis on the heroic literature of Homer, Aeschylus, Virgil, Dante, and Shakespeare in the chapter titled "Reading." Then compare the description of himself at work in his bean-field in the chapter titled "The Beanfield." He means for the reader to see a close vital connection between the heroic life and the rural, agrarian, pastoral life. It is a clear-cut illustration of the pattern of "Apollo as servant shepherd," of "Ajax cooking his dinner," of "Hercules cleansing the stable," of "Christ born in a manger, attended by shepherds," of "Chiron as high school science teacher." Furthermore, the pattern is as essential to the "American Dream" as Thomas Jefferson's theory of "natural aristocracy," which in itself may be seen as curiously related to pastoralism. Whitman's celebration of the "common man," rolling in the hay and contemplating the metaphysics of grass, is a version of Milon and Battus lounging in a shadowy glade, contemplating and singing the glory of Demeter.[22]

Finally, the consideration of heroic and pastoral patterns brings us to the very important matter of anti-pastoral or mock-pastoral. The serious or straight pastoral itself contains the seeds of the anti-pastoral. To imply that a lowly character is ennobled or elevated by his very simplicity and lowness borders on the comic; certainly the idea is ironic. It does not conform to the expected order of things, and it contains an apparent contradiction. And, after all, the very technique of elevating a lowly subject to epic or heroic heights is a basically comic technique—mock-epic. On the other hand, treating a lofty subject in a matter-of-fact or low way is burlesque.

It seems to me that a helpful distinction can be made

between mock-pastoral and anti-pastoral techniques, especially as they apply to modern fiction. The basis for both techniques is a fundamental questioning of that a priori assumption which says that the simple rural way of life is better than the urban, sophisticated way of life. The assumption becomes especially questionable when the pastoral way of life is consistently presented as superior to urban life, as it is, in fact, presented from Theocritus even down to the present in the serious pastoral. The pastoral attitude is fundamentally contrary to experience: that is, the open-eyed man will see that there are certain advantages to rural life, and there are certain advantages to urban life; there are good shepherds and farmers, and there are evil shepherds and farmers; "snowy flocks" may exist somewhere, but dirty, smelly sheep also exist (and, experientially, they exist in far greater abundance than snowy flocks). Thus, the very attitude and subject matter of the serious pastoral are vulnerable to satiric and ironic treatment from the very beginning.

Mock-pastoral, then, exists when the author (or character) embraces the basic assumptions of pastoralism and applies them to a seemingly suitable subject, and they do not work. This may as well apply to an idyllic notion of sexual love as to an idyllic love of the land and nature. It is mock-pastoral when the attitude and the subject matter will not fit the preconceived notions and conventions of the serious pastoral mode. Often this failure will depend in part upon a misunderstanding of the pastoral mode itself. For example, a character may fail to see that pastoralism is largely a convention—a sophisticated ideal, rather than an attainable and tenable reality. He may in all seriousness seek the pastoral ideal without understanding the mode, and, of course, he is doomed. Rightly treated, either laughter or pathos, or a combination of the two can result when this occurs—pathos and laughter when George Babbitt tries to escape to the Maine woods; pathos alone when Rabbit Angstrom tries to flee to gardening, the woods, and uninhibited sex; laughter when the simple shepherd/farmer turns out to be nothing more than a simpleminded bumpkin. (In fact, the long tradition of country bumpkins found in the American tradition can be related to a tradition of mock-pastoralism.)

Most of the possibilities of the mock-pastoral can be found in Shakespeare's *As You Like It*. There he has courtiers move into Arden Forest in pursuit of the pastoral way of life; but, it seems that *two* pastoral worlds exist— 1) the ideal, as conceived in the serious pastoral mode, and represented by the vapid, bloodless, and unrealistic Corin, Silvius, and Phebe, and 2) the real, as represented by the dirty, coarse, ignorant Audrey, William, and Sir Oliver Martext. Furthermore, the Duke Senior has managed actually to find a kind of meaning and solace in the forest, and he, like Thoreau, "Finds tongues in trees, books in the running brooks,/Sermons in stones and good in every thing" (act 2, scene 1). The play is anti-pastoral in that it challenges, refutes, and exposes the fallacies underlying the pastoral mode. It is mock-pastoral in that it employs the very assumptions and techniques of the serious pastoral to expose the mode. Significantly, *As You Like It* ends in a series of marriages (signifying a symbolic union between urban and rural, among other things), and a general return to the sophistication of the court.

The anti-pastoral mode can work in another way—still ironic, but tending less toward comedy. I mean that anti-pastoral can be *any* use of the pastoral attitude and subject matter in which pastoralism is set up as a norm against which life is measured or evaluated. This technique is especially important in twentieth-century fiction. In this particular use of pastoral, the pastoral ideal may in fact be a valid touchstone. More often, though, the pastoral becomes merely a dream, a symbol of loss, a reminder of past innocence—often a set of values, an innocence, a way of life which never really existed in the first place. The elemental, simple life in a state of nature becomes a part of the American Dream and agrarian myth as surely as "liberty and justice for all" and "frontier self-reliance" are a part of it. Thus, we have a whole pattern of modern short fiction and novels in which pastoral elements become either ironic touchstones and norms or patently spurious and dangerous lies. When the pastoralism becomes a touchstone, the motif is often associated with nostalgia, pathos, and even agonized longing—for youth, for nature, for Eden, for the Blessed Isles, for innocence, for lyricism and poetry—for all that is *idyllic*. And the idyllic, placed up against the waste-landish complexity of computerized, concretized urban sophistication, makes that harsh complexity and artificiality all the more terrible and painful. When the dream of the pastoral idyl is employed as a fatuously sought lie (usually by characters like Babbitt, or Rabbit Angstrom, unable to see or understand that from the beginning it was a sophisticated type of myth and legend), those characters tend to become absurd, laughable, pitiable grotesques.

The line between pastoral and anti-pastoral is obscured from the beginning by the relative sophistication underlying the pastoral prototype. In a sense, it would be safe to say that twentieth-century American life as a whole is "anti-pastoral"—in the sense that life today is essentially opposed to simple, rural, agrarian closeness to nature. But it seems that the farther Americans are removed from the soil (removed, for example, in the quite literal sense of high-rise apartments of steel, concrete, and glass), the more desperately they long for the pastoral idyl. Certainly in modern American literature the theme and technique have become extensive—extensive enough to merit a critical study like this, for instance.

If the pastoral motif does not dominate a work, still writers feel compelled to touch upon it by inserting a pastoral element—an element like Willy Loman's compulsion to get some seeds into the ground, his tragic *gesture* toward pastoralism. Like Falstaff "babbling of green fields" at his death, Loman makes an incoherent gesture toward Thoreau, Crèvecoeur, Milton, and all the pastoralists back to Theocritus, and even to the Garden of Eden. Like the first Alexandrian Greek authors of the pastoral, and like the sophisticated Virgil, writers (and characters) tend to flee to pastoralism when life becomes too confining, too constructing. As Willy Loman says while planting his final garden, "Where the hell is that seed? You can't see nothing out here! They boxed in the whole goddam neighborhood!" [23] Whether as an ironic contrast or as a viable goal, heroes of modern American fiction seek the pastoral—much in the way Oedipus sought it at Colonus. Even Herzog, Saul Bellow's defeated and tormented hero, flees to the parody of the pastoral idyl, the run-down, overgrown "summer house" he and his wife had bought in the country, with hopes of restoring it. These modern princes and heroes (like Herzog and Rabbit Angstrom and Willy Loman) have vague, undefined feelings about life in nature, but they lack the synthesizing imagination of Theocritus, Virgil, and Thoreau. Their attempts to return to nature are consistently thwarted or exposed as absurd—like the attempts of the courtiers in *As You Like It*.

In summary, the mock-pastoral and anti-pastoral modes work in two ways: 1) a parody or exposé of the pastoral life can reveal that life to be a dream-world or an unattainable and false ideal; 2) evocation of the serious pastoral can be a norm or touchstone against which sophisticated life is contrasted, resulting in an ironic devaluation of the seemingly superior sophistication. In the first sense, the basic a priori assumptions of the serious pastoral mode are questioned; in the second sense, the assumptions of urban sophistication are questioned, and emphasis is placed on the degree to which modern life is essentially opposed to and alienated from the pastoral way of life.

For a writer or character who sees real value in nature and a pastoral, agrarian way of life, a special problem exists: he must present his argument so that it does not appear funny in itself. Thus, he can perhaps follow Thoreau's course in *Walden*: he can laugh at his own position *before* anyone else has a chance to laugh at him. In *Walden* Thoreau draws his experiment at the pond in terms of an epic or heroic quest; but the very simplicity and rusticity of his way of living is so obviously *un*heroic and *un*sophisticated in its externals that the very incongruity evokes smiles. So, Thoreau smiles *first* by including those im-

portant mock-epic elements scattered throughout his book
—the Odyssean mosquito, the famous ant battle, the mock-
heroic attack on the army of weeds in the beanfield, the
attack on the locomotive-dragon with the writing-pen
lance. The mock-epic elements free Thoreau to discuss his
altogether serious heroic *spiritual* quest in serious terms.
Updike seems to know this trick of laughing first, in order
to clear the air for serious heroism. For instance, the outright absurdity of equating a high school girls' gym teacher
with Aphrodite, a lecherous high school principal with Zeus,
and a drunken bum with Bacchus clears the way for
equating a young artist with Prometheus, and his farm-
oriented mother with Ceres. By the end of both *Walden*
and *The Centaur*, nobody laughs; rather, we are stirred by
a sense of the grand, the eloquent, and the heroic.

The pastoral mode is characterized by artistic boldness
more than any other trait. It is a bold stroke when Milton
turns Edward King into "Lycidas," when Matthew Arnold
turns Arthur Hugh Clough into "Thyrsis." Interestingly
enough, it is a kind of reversal of the boldness of the
original Greek and Latin pattern of turning realistically
rough shepherds into elegant, eloquent singers and poets.
It is this boldness, this striking artistic effect, I take it,
which Samuel Johnson so objected to in Milton's pastoral elegy. But, is it not essentially the same kind of metaphoric boldness we find when John Updike compares the
science teacher Caldwell to Chiron, or when he includes
an ironic, idyllic love lyric, complete with stock images and
language, in the middle of a realistic story about plane-
stranded *New Yorker* adulterers? Critics have commented
on Updike's tendency to use idyllic, poetic language from
the beginning; but for some reason they have failed to
see that that particular kind of language is related to his
central theme—pastoral and anti-pastoral in our time. The
Greek and Latin pastoralists elevate simple shepherds and
rustics into dignified, heroic characters; so do modern
British and American fiction writers. A similar attitude underlies both the Greek *Idyls* and *The Centaur*, as surely as it
underlies *Ulysses* and *The Centaur*. An attitude, a subject,

a technique—employed in complex variations by Shakespeare, and extending into our own time as versions of pastoral and anti-pastoral—these are the matters to be discussed in greater detail in the following chapters of this essay.

2

Versions of Pastoral and Anti-Pastoral Patterns in the American Tradition

Having broadly defined and generally examined the pastoral and anti-pastoral modes in the preceding chapter, I feel that some further examination of specific uses of the modes will be useful, before I begin a detailed analysis of John Updike's employment of the pattern. My thesis, after all, is not merely that John Updike makes use of the pattern, but also that the pattern exists as a strong, historically traceable current in the American literary tradition. Furthermore, for a writer as acutely aware of his literary and intellectual heritage as John Updike is, to see his art outside of the traditions on which it is based is to miss much of the point. For Updike, the past intrudes into the present with a power more like a reincarnation than an apparition; it thrusts itself into his characters' minds and lives with a special force—the way those lyrically poetic passages in his prose abruptly shift the tone of a story and startle the reader or make him slow down to consider the power of individual words and images, as if they were words and images in a poem.

Probably no other modern writer of fiction, with the exception of William Faulkner, so strongly bases his themes on past traditions and cultural patterns as John Updike does. True, for both Updike and Faulkner, emphasis is on loss; but, to see clearly *what* has been lost (whether it is a corrupt but functional code of chivalry in Faulkner, or a set of rural, transcendental values in Updike), is one way of reconciling oneself to that loss. Often Updike's (and

Faulkner's) bewildered, questing characters become alien-ated and frustrated precisely because they cannot see and understand truths about past traditions and patterns, and consequently cannot reconcile and integrate those tradi-tions into their present lives. This is largely Rabbit Angstrom's problem in his attempt to "return to nature." We feel that, had he known more about the history of such attempts in the American tradition, perhaps he would not have striven so fervently, and failed so utterly in his attempt.

For the literary critic to discuss an author's work without seeing that work in its historical context—that is, for ex-ample, to discuss pastoralism in Updike's work without commenting on earlier versions of pastoralism—is to miss an important dimension of the work, the historical di-mension. True, there is some value in the now old "new critical" notion that a work should be analyzed in relative isolation from other works; but it is a notion that at best works for some poetry, often fails for prose, and at worst ends in semantic sophistry for both. It is rather like an historian's talking about the Great Depression of the thirties without also talking about the causes of that Depression inherent in the economic history of the twenties. Perhaps the literary critics' recent emphasis on archetypes and his-torical patterns is a reaction to the misuse and failure of "new critical" techniques. So far as I can tell, it is tre-mendously important that both Henry David Thoreau, Rabbit Angstrom, and a whole group of characters in Up-dike's short stories attempted versions of a "return to nature." It is equally important that in chapter nineteen of *Huckleberry Finn*, Huck uses a special type of poetic and idyllic language to describe life on the raft; and John Updike uses a similar type of language, also poetic and idyllic, in certain chapters of *The Centaur*.

This chapter, then, will serve as a brief survey of some of the outstanding examples of versions of pastoralism in the American tradition. I shall especially emphasize anti-pastoralism, since that topic has been notably slighted in most previous discussions of the pastoral mode in American literature.[1] Because Updike and other twentieth-century artists have inherited the tradition (much in the way they have inherited elements of Puritanism and transcendentalism), I shall divide my discussion into three general parts: the Puritan legacy, the transcendental legacy, and the twentieth-century beneficiaries. Two important points should be kept in the reader's mind: 1) Like any brief historical survey, the discussion will necessarily be incomplete, focusing on representative works and authors. 2) My usage of the terms *pastoral* and *anti-pastoral* includes considerably more meaning than the mere treatment of a genre or an Arcadian myth; it includes all those implications of an attitude and a subject matter, as I have outlined them in the preceding chapter.

First, the Puritan legacy. The New England contemporaries Thomas Morton and William Bradford, temperamentally and philosophically opposites and enemies, may be singled out as symbolically significant to a discussion of pastoral and anti-pastoral traditions in American literature. In fact, the writings of these two earliest New England colonists (Bradford arrived in 1620, Morton in 1622) clearly establish not only distinctive attitudes toward nature and the new land of America, but also distinctive literary styles—attitudes and styles which can be traced even down to the present time. Morton's short but important *New English Canaan* is pure pastoralism in the strongest Theocritan tradition—from its basic idealized vision to its specialized type of poetic, idyllic language. The description of the New England landscape is linguistically far removed from the harsh realism we find in Bradford's tough-minded, clear "plain style." In *The New English Canaan*, with its "sweet crystal fountains," its "streams that twine in fine meanders through the meads," its "turtle doves on the green boughs," its "lilies and Daphne-trees," we encounter a prose poem—stockly phrased, removed from reality, and self-consciously poetic. The sea becomes "Neptune's Court"; knolls become "dainty fine round rising hillocks"; branches become "arms that bend." Complete with belabored assonance and alliteration, the diction is poetic and idyllic.[2] Morton's work is pastoral, poetically celebrating lushness, tranquility, natural opulence—Dionysian, sophisticated, amorous about nature. Song birds and fruit. Murmuring fountains. Paradisaical summer. A scene that "lulls the sense with delight asleep." The Garden of Eden. Morton is like Shakespeare's Duke Senior who "Finds tongues in trees, books in running brooks,/ Sermons in stones and good in every thing" (*As You Like It*, act 2, scene 1).

Thus, from the very beginning of American colonization till the present—from John Smith's perfumed aristocrats in Virginia, to Thomas Morton's maypoling hedonists in New England, to Nathaniel Hawthorne's idealistic intellectuals at Blithedale Farm, to John Updike's fornicating couples in pastoral Tarbox, Massachusetts—a strong line of pastoral and anti-pastoral psychology persists. The *New English Canaan* suggests a main current in the historical pattern—a stream of thinking which identifies a return to nature with a return to a pre-lapsarian Eden, innocence, and sensuality, as opposed to the strict intellectuality and spirituality of Puritanism.

Geographically, Morton's pastoral Merry Mount, Massachusetts (1622) cannot have been very far removed from John Updike's fictional Tarbox, Massachusetts (1968). Ideologically, Morton's maypole may well have occupied the very center of Updike's "Tarbox Green"! And as William Bradford and the Plymouth colonists felt compelled to chastise and condemn the pagan and pastoral May Day celebrations of Merry Mount, so Updike in *Couples* exposes and condemns the grossly promiscuous and pointless sexuality and adultery of the twentieth-century Massachusetts nymphs and satyrs. In different ways, then, both colonial Puritanism and John Updike's *Couples* are "anti-pastoral." The difference is that Updike is critically cautionary and obliquely moralistic; Bradford is deadly serious in his militant opposition to paganism.

My point is that Puritanism itself, despite its own type of myth-making and its penchant for Old Testament analogies and metaphors, is essentially anti-pastoral in its realistic attitude toward the land, and toward the hard cold realities of poor people struggling to survive. No nymphs and satyrs and shadowy groves and murmuring fountains meandering through meads for the Plymouth settlers. One need only compare Bradford's and Morton's descriptions of the Massachusetts landscape. The difference lies in the attitudes and styles. Bradford emphasizes the desolation, danger, fear, and wildness of the place. He sees things as they are, without idealizing them either in his mind or in his language. Instead of "goodly groves" with "bowing arms," he sees "woods and thickets." Instead of "nature's masterpiece," he sees "a hideous and desolate wilderness." He is impressed by the wildness of the place, "wild beasts and wild men," and "the wild and savage hue." [3] His clarity of vision—his "realism"—becomes anti-pastoral when placed up against the obviously pastoral style of Morton. Rather than a scene that "lulls the sense with delight asleep," Bradford sees a disordered wilderness that must be tamed.

William Bradford's anti-pastoralism—and the basic brand of American Puritan opposition to pastoralism itself—is probably best illustrated in his direct condemnation of Morton and the maypole festivities at Merry Mount. In his indictment, he lists poetry, drinking, dancing, sexual intercourse, and celebratory nature rites as the major sins of the Merry Mount "Bacchanalians." These elements are all important parts of the prototypic Greek pastoral mode; Theocritan Idyls are sensual, sexual, and even licentious. Consider Bradford's condemnation of Morton's Arcadians:

They also set up a maypole, drinking and dancing about it many days together, inviting the Indian women for their consorts, dancing and frisking together like so many fairies, or furies, rather; and worse practices. As if they had anew revived and celebrated the feasts of the Roman goddess Flora, or the beastly practices of the mad Bacchanalians. Morton likewise, to show his poetry composed sundry rhymes and verses, some tending to lasciviousness, and others to the detraction and scandal of some persons, which he affixed to this idle or idol maypole. They changed also the name of their place, and instead of calling it Mount Wollaston they call it Merry-mount, as if this jollity would have lasted ever. [4]

Note that in this clearly anti-pastoral attitude even Bradford resorts to a couple of rare and crude attempts at puns (*fairies* and *furies, idle* and *idol*) —suggestive that the anti-pastoral mode as a style tends toward satire and irony.

The implications of Bradford's attack on pastoralism later become highly serious: the idyllic view of the world espoused by Morton and his crew subsequently results in dangerous armament of the Indians, in bloodshed, and in disorder. Pastoralism becomes associated with chaos and terror. The anti-pastoralist insists that "this jollity cannot last forever." Courtiers must leave Arden Forest and return to the court, as indeed Morton, as an outlaw, later fled back to England. Thoreau must leave Walden Pond. Brook Farm experiments pitifully peter out. In John Updike's *Couples*, the couples have originally fled to rural, pastoral Tarbox to enjoy trees and beaches and unconfined simplicity, including sexual freedom. Their idyl works for a while, but like the Merry Mount experience, it ends in disaster—neglected children, adultery, perversion, divorce, abortion, death, and chaos. It is no accident that several of Updike's couples live in restored colonial houses, and that the Tarbox church dates back to colonial times. The important point here seems to be that the pastoral attitude and way of life have been a part of the American tradition from the very beginning. But whenever anyone tries to impose the pastoral ideal on real life, he is doomed to failure. It must remain an ideal, an idea, a mode, a poetic imagining in order to retain its validity.

The Puritan legacy, then, is essentially anti-pastoralism and tough-minded realism. The Puritan attitude toward nature is to subdue, Christianize, and civilize it. Indians are not "noble savages" to be taken as "consorts"; rather, they are "wild men," to be clothed, catechized, and pushed into the forest. On the other hand, the Merry Mount pastoralists see nature as subject matter for poetry, as a setting for erecting maypoles, as a grove and glen to be free, emancipated, and licentious in. Both attitudes still exist to varying degrees, and both attitudes receive prominent attention in the pastoral and anti-pastoral patterns of John Updike's fiction.

After Puritanism, the next great ideological legacy bequeathed to twentieth-century America was transcendentalism. Eccles, the Episcopalian clergyman in *Rabbit, Run,* is the heir of his New England grandfather's liberal transcendentalism—of the Emersonian tradition which suggested that God was in the woods, not behind stained glass windows. Romantic transcendentalism of the nineteenth century, with its emphasis on man's goodness and perfectibility in a state of nature, rests on a foundation of classical pastoralism. Indeed, the entire pattern of American agrarianism, democratic ideals, and transcendental religious values can be related to a curious version of the Theocritan tradition.

The entire body of transcendental concepts originated before 1800. Even the influential Rousseauistic primitivism, refined and Americanized into Jeffersonian democratic idealism, can be seen as a version of the basic attitude of the Theocritan pastoral. Who are Jefferson's "natural aristocrats" but those noble, simple Theocritan and Virgilian shepherds of the *Idyls,* the *Eclogues,* and the *Georgics?* Simultaneously, while the corrupt, fated, terminal French courtiers of Louis XVI artificially played at being pastoral milkmaids and shepherds at Versailles (like the unreal shepherds in *As You Like It,* and like the frisking maypolers at Merry Mount), Thomas Jefferson worked at founding a government to celebrate and perpetuate the nobility and dignity of real farmers and herdsmen—the gargantuan and faceless "American common man." Part of the pattern seems to be the premise that simplicity implies nobility—bucolic closeness to the earth implies ennoblement and spiritual aggrandisement. As V. L. Parrington says of the movement,

Since the great desideratum is man in a state of nature, it follows, according to the Physiocratic school, that the farmer is the ideal citizen, and agriculture the common and single source of wealth; and that in consequence the state should hold the tillers of the soil in special regard, shaping the public policy with a primary view to their interests.[5]

Without saying it outright, Parrington sums up the era's proximity to the classical pastoral assumption, complete with the *moral* judgment that farming and farmers are superior to urbanized sophisticates. Edward William Taylor, although primarily concerned with the tension between Nature and Art, comments on the "definable moral dimension" of pastoralism:

Pastoral idealizes the original condition of man, or at least what it represents to be man's original condition; like the myth of the Golden Age, which it embodied almost from the first and later assimilated to its own purposes, the pastoral generally conveys formal nostalgia for a lost time of happiness and natural simplicity. Thus its potentiality for moral assertion is, in a sense, built in. . . . Pastoral has, therefore, a satirical reflex, and possesses, despite its reputation to the contrary, a definable moral dimension. As God preferred the shepherd Abel before Cain, symbolizing the superiority of the contemplative to the active life, so pastoral prefers Nature to Art.[6]

These moral assumptions, inherent in Jeffersonian democracy and historically traceable back to the *Idyls* and to Vergil's *Eclogues* and *Georgics*, profoundly influenced American letters for the greater part ot the nineteenth century. Thus, agrarianism, return to nature, and *Original Innocence* (that is, the pastoral values) come into conflict with the civilization, urbanization, and *Original Sin* of the Puritan heritage (that is, the anti-pastoral values). Certain major works of this period, especially those of Emerson, Thoreau, and Hawthorne, must, it seems to me, be seen in terms of pastoral and anti-pastoral patterns. That is, the works largely exist as a result of the dramatic tension produced by the innocent-sinful, rural-urban, simple-sophisticated, lyric-prosaic dichotomies.

One of the literary historians to clearly see the early significance of pastoralism in the American tradition is Daniel G. Hoffman. In his excellent study, *Form and Fable in American Fiction*, he discusses the appearance of the "bumpkin servant" and the "noble rustic hero" which appeared as early as Royal Tyler's *The Contrast* (1787). Hoffman says that by 1820 the Yankee countryman "now plays a *version of Pastoral*, in which he possesses the limitless wisdom of his motherwit." [7] Hoffman discusses this character type as follows:

The usual pattern of one numerous genre of the American novel is to move an innocent character from his country home into the temptations and evils of city life. This pattern conforms not only to that found in the "young man from the province" class of novels, but also to the movement of populations in the American nineteenth and twentieth centuries.[8]

Consider the extent to which John Updike's fiction—especially *The Centaur*, with its country-city tensions, and *Couples*, with its village "nymphs and satyrs" (Updike's term)—fits into the pattern Hoffman describes above. Small wonder that Updike described his sophisticated editorial "we" of the *New Yorker*'s "Talk of the Town" as "a collection of dazzled farm boys." Consider the telling extent to which both Updike and his characters are innocently "moved from their country homes into the temptations and evils of city life." Much of the anguish of John Updike's characters—both spiritual and emotional—is closely related to the anguish of the kind experienced by Robin (the displaced pastoral hero) in Nathaniel Hawthorne's story, "My Kinsman, Major Molineux."

Pastoral and anti-pastoral patterns are especially applicable to the major writers of the American Renaissance: Emerson, Thoreau, and Whitman; Hawthorne, Melville, and Poe. The six writers may conveniently be classed into two groups, positive romanticists and negative romanticists. For practical purposes of gauging intellectual currents and techniques, the terms *positive* and *negative* are helpful. Emerson, Thoreau, and Whitman are "positive" in that they all affirm the basic benevolence and meaningfulness of the universe; furthermore, they emphasize Nature as good, instructive, moral, and symbolically positive. Hawthorne, Melville, and Poe are "negative" in that they consistently question the benevolence and meaningfulness of the universe; in contrast to the positivists, Hawthorne, Melville, and Poe emphasize Nature as often evil, malevolent, amoral, perversely accidental, ambiguous, obscure, and negative.

Now, the significant point here is that the basic assumptions of Emerson, Thoreau, and Whitman are essentially the same as those of Theocritus, Virgil, Thomas Morton, Crèvecoeur, Freneau, Jefferson, Bryant, Cooper—that is, they are pastoral, agrarian, Rousseauan. On the other hand, it is significant that works like *The Blithedale Romance, Typee, Omoo, Moby Dick,* and Poe's short stories all question the benevolence of Nature, question the dream of a return to innocence and nature, question the basic goodness and simplicity of man and the universe—that is, they are anti-pastoral. Correspondingly, these negativistic writers have failed to arrive at the utterance of Carlyle's "everlasting Yea," which in itself can be significantly related to the basic universal affirmation inherent in the pastoral attitude.

Peripherally significant at this point is the importance of the Christian vision in relation to pastoral and anti-pastoral elements of American romanticism and transcendentalism. Ironically, despite the traditional Christian emphasis on humble simplicity, "the Good Shepherd," and "the lilies of the field," it is the positivists (Emerson, Thoreau, and Whitman) who are farthest removed from orthodox Christian doctrine, and who are most heretical. A little like Thomas Morton, they suggest that a new Eden—a kind of spiritual Merry Mount or Christian idyl —can exist *in this world*. They gaze back to the Garden of Eden rather than forward to the Christian heaven, reminiscent of Theocritus gazing back from the Alexandrian court to the pastoral simplicity of the Arcadian hills of his youth. On the other hand, Hawthorne, Melville, and Poe (preoccupied with malevolence, sin, and evil like those original Plymouth Puritans who chopped down the Merry Mount maypole), are strangely orthodox (in a Manichaean way) in their emphasis on the primary Christian fact that "we are all sinners." The transcendental positivists in America (with their technically heretical dogma that man is basically *good* and capable of saving *himself* through individual spiritual transcendence) may well be the most influential figures in effecting the downfall of traditional Christianity as we know it in the twentieth century. This theme of the failure of Christianity in our time is a major concern in John Updike's fiction—for instance, Rabbit Angstrom of *Rabbit, Run,* George Caldwell of *The Centaur,* and Piet Hanema of *Couples* all have a kind of desperate Christian faith. In the cases of Rabbit Angstrom and Piet Hanema, the faith pitifully fails because it is all confused with a transcendental (i.e., an essentially pastoral and curiously pagan) version of Christianity.

As Shakespeare showed in *As You Like It,* as Bradford illustrated in *Of Plymouth Plantation,* as John Milton theologized in *Paradise Lost,* as Melville showed in *Moby Dick* and *Typee,* as Hawthorne showed in *The Blithedale Romance,* and as a whole group of twentieth-century authors have illustrated, the pastoral transcendental dream of salvation by purely human means is doomed to failure. The dream becomes recklessly dangerous when applied to real life and confused with reality. The attempt to be saved by returning to nature, innocence, and Eden becomes a kind of pride—in Christian theology the deadliest of all the sins. Compared to the orthodoxy of *Billy Budd, Nature* is sheer heresy: Herman Melville—not Ralph Waldo Emerson—wrote *Billy Budd.*

Ralph Waldo Emerson works directly in the pastoral tradition. Like the authors of the Greek idyls and the Roman eclogues, he is a sophisticated, erudite intellectual who asserts that the answers to man's existential conflicts and dilemmas can be found in a return to the simplicity and order of nature. Emerson's theme, tone, and diction in *Nature* (1836) is a reflection of the celebratory Theocritan mode, with its emphasis on "perfect exhilaration," "the woods," "perpetual youth," "perennial festivals," and "tranquil landscapes." When Emerson asserts that "In the woods, too, a man casts off his years, as the snake his slough, and at what period soever of life, is always a child," he aligns himself with the Greek and Roman pastoralists as surely as he aligns himself with pre-lapsarian Adamists, Rousseauan primitivists, and Wordsworthian child cultists.

Emerson considers nature first of all a "setting" for man; like the classical pastoralist, he is more interested in "man in nature" than in nature for its own sake. That Emerson found the wilderness "dear and connate" should be contrasted to the fact that the Puritan William Bradford had earlier found the wilderness "hideous and desolate." It was Thomas Morton, the Merry Mount pastoralist, who had celebrated the wilderness as "paradise" and "nature's masterpiece." Emerson's references to "the frolic of the nymphs" and to "a perennial festival" represent those peculiar dictional sign posts which doggedly accompany the pastoral attitude and style.[9] Even Emerson's assertion that "Nature always wears the colors of the spirit" recalls the fact that the original pastoral mode included the pastoral elegy and lament, as well as the pastoral love lyric and harvest song. Emerson, in rejecting the church and espousing the woods, essentially rejected Original Sin and espoused a doctrine of Original Innocence—heresy in Christian terms, and an orthodoxly fundamental manuever in the pastoral pattern.

In Emerson's transcendentalism, men are not so much fallen sinners hoping and working for redemption, as they are merely unrealized potential Adams: Eden and Arcady await us in the woods. Rather like John Updike's influential modern philosopher in *Rabbit, Run* (ironically, that philosopher is "Jimmy, the Big Mouseketeer" of a children's television program), Emerson emphasizes *being* rather than *knowing*. Emerson, like the "Big Mouseketeer," essentially twists the maxim *"know* thyself" into *"be* yourself."[10] There is a big difference between the two admonitions—the difference between Adam before The Fall (a state of being) and Adam after The Fall (a state of knowing). Despite the intervention of a hundred and fifty years since the writing of *Nature*, Emersonian transcendentalism still exists in America as an influential force—as witnessed, for example, by the number of characters in John Updike's fiction who attempt an Emersonian "return to nature." Like Emerson himself, Updike's heroes begin with orthodox faith, reject it, and attempt individual transcendence. Unlike Emerson, these modern *self*-reliant questers (such as Updike's Rabbit Angstrom, Piet Hanema, and "The Hermit," as opposed to *god*-reliant conservatives like his Caldwell-Centaur) miserably fail in their simplistic pastoral attempts. Historically, the anti-pastoral pattern of failure can be traced back to the failure of the Merry Mount attempt with its "frisking and worse," especially since uninhibited sexuality (inherent in Theocritus, symbolic in Christian orthodoxy, and rather old-maidishly overlooked in Emerson and Thoreau) is part of the pre-lapsarian pastoral dream. Significantly, Updike's wildly fornicating would-be swains (Angstrom and Hanema) evolve, at best, as rather pitiable and destructive anti-heroes, whereas his most patently heroic character, George Caldwell-Centaur, sums up his anti-pastoral attitude toward nature as follows: "Cassie, I want to be frank with you, because you're my wife. I hate Nature. It reminds me of death. All Nature means to me is garbage and confusion and the stink of skunk—brroo!" [11]

As Walt Whitman extended Emerson's coolly intellectual transcendentalism into spiritually and physically passionate nature-worship, several of Updike's characters are strikingly (and dangerously) Whitmanesque. The "I" of *Song of Myself* (that extraordinarily sensitive proletarian lounging on the grass, rolling in the hay, and orgiastically coupling with lovers and comrades and winds and seas), has a spiritual ancestor in the shepherd-swain of the classical pastoral mode.[12] And he has a spiritual descendent in Rabbit Angstrom, in Piet Hanema, and in Stanley of Updike's short story "The Hermit."

Thoreau understood the sophisticated assumptions behind pastoralism. He makes it clear that the Walden experiment is just that—an experiment. He is careful not to recommend it as a coda, or guidebook, or a way of life for other men; and he himself explains why he left the woods. He does not make the mistake of believing that the Walden experience could (or should) last forever. Probably the greatest error a reader of *Walden* can make is to see it as a practical guidebook to living—an error comparable to using the Theocritan *Idyls* as a text on animal husbandry, or the Homeric epics as texts on military strategy. Unfortunately, this misinterpretation of *Walden* has been so widespread that Thoreau would shudder at some of the effects of his poetic work. (I am thinking especially of, say, twentieth-century hippies and flower children who have appropriated Thoreau to their own naïve philosophy without understanding either the art or the traditions of his work.) He who reads *Walden* without first reading Homer *and* Theocritus is sure to miss much of the point. Thoreau does idealize in the traditional pastoral way; and it is his very sophistication and erudition which save his work from absurdity and disaster. When an uneducated and unsophisticated janitor in John Updike's short story "The Hermit" (published as the last story in the collection *The Music School*) tries a twentieth-century Thoreauvian escape to asceticism in the woods, his quest ends in devastating failure: he is considered a madman, and he is taken away from his cabin to be committed to an asylum.

Pastoralism, like all ideals of human and social perfection (and all "Utopias" and "Blessed Isles") must remain a dream and an ideal to remain valid. This seems to be at least part of Thoreau's conclusion in *Walden*, that any single system or dogma or code is unsatisfactory in the face of the multiplicity and complexity of life itself. This includes pastoralism, or any other *ism*. Like Thoreau's "beaten track" from his cabin door to the pond-side, "the ruts of tradition and conformity," of pastoralism and primitivism, are just as confining as any other ruts.[13] Thus, Thoreau is perhaps as closely related to anti-pastoralism as to pastoralism, despite the popular misconceptions about his work. His own comments from his *Journal* (November 19, 1843, entry), are helpful in placing him in the tradition:

Pastoral poetry belongs to a highly civilized and refined era. It is the pasture as seen from the hall window—the shepherd of the manor. Its sheep are never actually shorn nor die of the rot. The towering, misty imagination of the poet has descended into the plain and become a lowlander, and keeps flocks and herds. Between the hunting of men and boars and the feeding of sheep is a long interval. Really the shepherd's pipe is no wax-compacted reed, but made of pipe-clay, and nothing but smoke issues from it. Nowadays the sheep take care of themselves for the most part.[14]

There can be little doubt as to where Thoreau would have
placed himself in terms of pastoral and anti-pastoral patterns. Likewise, there can be little doubt as to his actual
position in the American pattern.

Although Herman Melville and Nathaniel Hawthorne
are both related to pastoral and anti-pastoral traditions, it is
perhaps Hawthorne who stands out as one of the most significant Americans to deal with pastoral values in the nineteenth century. Although one could profitably concentrate
on works such as Melville's *Typee* and *Omoo* as versions of
pastoral, it is probably most fruitful to comment on Hawthorne's "The Maypole of Merry Mount" and *The Blithedale Romance* as representative examples of pastoral and
anti-pastoral attitudes.

Over two hundred years after William Bradford wrote his
account of the Merry Mount incident, Nathaniel Hawthorne
wrote a fictionalized account of the affair. In the story, pastoral and anti-pastoral values dramatically clash.[15] Perhaps
the most significant fact about this story is that the conflict
between the two sets of values was still viable in Hawthorne's
time—timely and consuming enough for Hawthorne to feel
the need to write the story. Daniel G. Hoffman, in *Form
and Fable in American Fiction*, has traced those peculiarly
pastoral elements in the story: the "Lord and Lady of the
May," the garlands of flowers, the maypole masque, the
"pipe, cithern, and viol, touched with practised minstrelsy,"
and all the other pastoral machinery.[16] Hoffman quotes from
the story and comments:

They are introduced as a "wild throng" of "Gothic monsters,
though perhaps of Grecian ancestry"; "It could not be that the
fauns and nymphs, when driven from their classic groves and
homes of ancient fable, had sought refuge as all the persecuted
did, in the fresh woods of the West." How ambiguous the implications! The masquers are allied with "the persecuted"—
not only with Quakers and Antinomians like Roger Williams
and Anne Hutchinson but with the Puritans themselves—who
seek refuge in "the fresh woods of the West." [17]

Pointing out that Hawthorne resolves the story by having
Endicott bestow mercy on the pastoral revelers, Hoffman

concludes that Hawthorne's "own soul is in both camps." If we can accept this evaluation of Hawthorne's position—and I think it is a valid conclusion in terms of the story itself—then we have in Hawthorne a version of the anti-pastoralist who longs to be a pastoralist. This figure is very important in understanding John Updike and other twentieth-century authors, for the basic pattern in fiction of our time involves just this tension—characters and authors who find the pastoral dream forcefully attractive, but who must reject it because of the even more forceful and imposing realities of modern civilization itself. Like Edgar and Edith (Adam and Eve?) of Hawthorne's story, twentieth-century nymphs and satyrs must succumb to the sheer power of jet transportation, television, automation, bureaucracies, and gadgets as surely as "the Lord and Lady of the May" had to submit to the power of the swords and muskets of the Puritan militants. We recall the pastoral dream of the stranded couple in Updike's "The Wait," where outside the Washington, D. C., airport the characters dream of "the fresh woods of the West" "in Wyoming, with . . . children, and a horse, and a cold little lake we can swim in, and a garden we can make near the house." The idyllic love lyric, even when it is a lament, strikes a chord which is necessary to complete the fragmenting effect of either grim Puritanism or stainless steel technology.

Their [Puritan] virtues Endicott names in granting pardon to Edgar and Edith: courage, sobriety, piety. But if the Merry-mounters, "sworn triflers of a lifetime," lacked the moral energy of Puritanism, the Puritans as surely lacked the spirit of love in which the Maypole had its roots. Because neither of these rival factions of mankind has the virtues of the other to compensate for its own defects, Hawthorne does not permit us to accept wholeheartedly the partial truth which either side represents.[18]

If Hawthorne's "own soul is in both camps" in "The Maypole of Merry Mount," he has assuredly defected to the anti-pastoral side in *Blithedale Romance*. In *The American Novel and Its Tradition*, Richard Chase says, "In a literature rich in pastoral idyls, *The Blithedale Romance* is one of the few anti-pastorals." [19] And in *Hawthorne's Tragic Vision*, Roy R. Male titles his chapter on the novel "The Anti-Pastoral Wasteland." Daniel G. Hoffman says of Hawthorne's romance:

The essential tensions in any pastoral work derive from the contrast between the "pastoral idyl" and "real life." The pastoral genre invites a comparison between the actual—the corrupted realm of necessity—and a bucolic image of perfection. In any anti-pastoral these contrasts are likely to be more explicit than implied, and to work to the disadvantage of the claims of perfection made for the bucolic idyl. For surely the best way to attack the idea of pastoral is to subject it to the same scrutiny which we usually give to the life of the real world.[20]

Thus, *The Blithedale Romance*, by testing and questioning the pastoral idealism behind such efforts as Brook Farm, becomes an important predecessor of a whole group of explicitly anti-pastoral fiction in the American tradition. The work is based on the irony inherent in the discrepancy between the ideal and the real—a theme inherent in the prototypic Theocritan idyl, pervasive in almost all of Shakespeare's work, and as contemporary as John Updike's *Couples*. And like the suburban characters in *Couples*, the Blithedale pastoralists specialize in masquerades:

Yet all at Blithedale are vulnerable to [Westervelt's] parody of their ideals, since they, like him, are portmanteau figures too. Each of the colonists, to dig new crops in Eden, has cast off his prior life like a wornout cloak and becomes an Arcadian, tending the pigs, mixing the gruel, supervising laundry. Their perpetual masquerade hides their true identities from one another.[21]

In the preceding quotation, substitute *Tarbox* for *Blithedale*, *Freddy Thorne* for *Westervelt*, *bar* for *pigs*, *martinis* for *gruel*, and *parties* for *laundry*, and the sentence applies as well to *Couples* as to *The Blithedale Romance*.

In summary, the transcendental and romantic pastoral and anti-pastoral legacy is one of the richest patterns in American literature. I have briefly sketched the tradition here, and further inquiry would reveal even further richness. For example, I have touched only on major writers of the period; the reader need only consider minor authors of the era (writers like Longfellow, Whittier, Holmes, and the minor regionalists) to grasp the extent to which the assumptions of pastoralism pervaded American literature of the period. Often accompanied by sentimentalism and bucolic posturings, the attitudes and techniques of pastoralism achieved striking popularity in the nineteenth century. Often rendered into execrable nationalistic treacle, the attitudes accompanied the rise of what we now refer to as the "agrarian myth," which ranges from "barefoot boy with cheek of tan" to *Evangeline* to *Hiawatha* to Horatio Alger stories. Perhaps the less said of these establishmentarian idyls, the better. The fact remains that the twentieth century had been awarded a legacy. And, like faded Sunday school cards, pressed flowers in old diaries, embroidered mottos, horse collars, frontier self-reliance, and Christianity itself, we didn't quite know what to do with the inheritance. We felt guilty in throwing it away; we found it a useless encumbrance around internal combustion engines and dynamos and atomic bombs; and it kept boomeranging back when we did try to junk it. What some representative modern novelists— the twentieth-century beneficiaries—have done with the pattern is the subject of the next portion of this essay.

Of the various directions of intellectual concerns in the American novel since 1900, pastoralism and anti-pastoralism constitute two strong currents. Mark Twain, accredited by Ernest Hemingway with founding modern American literature by writing *Huckleberry Finn*, had himself written a few idyls before the turn of the century. Tom Sawyer, if not exactly an elegant swain, was a representative of a lost youth and a lost time, in which simple childhood values had a kind of primitive grace and humor which could never again be regained in a corrupt adult world. Described by Twain as "simply a hymn put into prose form to give it a worldly air," [22] *Tom Sawyer* is reminiscent of the Theocritan pattern in which the sophisticated poet imaginatively recreates his Arcadian youth with longing and nostalgia. It is the kind of longing and nostalgia found in John Updike's short story collections *The Same Door* and *Olinger Stories*, which deal with childhood and high school experiences of a boy and his family in the small, pastoral town of Olinger, Pennsylvania (in reality, Updike's birthplace and schoolboy home, Shillington, Pennsylvania). That highly sophisticated, first-ranking authors like Mark Twain and John Updike should write these poignantly nostalgic and idyllic boyhood stories suggests that the pastoral attitude is often ingrained in the vision of our best and most complex writers. Twain, cynically realistic and pessimistic, looked homeward to the lost pastoral Hannibal; Updike, erudite, polished, realistic, and similarly cynical, looks homeward to the lost pastoral Shillington.

By 1885, the publication date of *Huckleberry Finn,* Twain had arrived at the point where he used idyllic lyricism as a foil or norm, against which he juxtaposed the violence, corruption, and hypocrisy of an adult and sophisticated world. In short, we see Twain still longing for innocence and simplicity, but unwilling to base a book on it, as he had done earlier in *Tom Sawyer.* The famous idyllic chapter nineteen in *Huckleberry Finn*—which begins with "Two or three days and nights went by; I reckon I might say they swum by, they slid along so quiet and smooth and lovely," which proceeds to describe life on the raft in pastorally poetic imagery, and which is summarized in the conclusion, "It's lovely to live on a raft"—is an interlude sandwiched in between the bloody Grangerford-Shepherdson feud, and the arrival of the Duke and the Dauphin on the raft. Perhaps a peripheral commentary on pastorally oriented "granges" and "shepherds," the chapter is much more. In a way, the chapter is a valediction to the very dreams of Edenic innocence—an evocation of the idyllic which renders corrupt reality all the more terrible. The ephemeral transitoriness of Huck and Jim's "return to nature" is as much a negation of the entire transcendental vision as it is a touchstone for making a sin-black society even uglier in contrast to it. Huck's moral growth is based on knowledge rather than innocence—a curiously Miltonic and orthodox version of the *Felix Culpa*: in order to make right moral decisions, man must know and confront evil, rather than seek sanctuary in blindness and innocence, even if that sanctuary consists in an extremely attractive pastoral dream of a return to nature. Like John Milton, Twain could not praise "a fugitive and cloistered virtue" such as the pastoral sanctuary. In a sense, *Huckleberry Finn* is as much of an anti-pastoral as *The Blithedale Romance* is, and the satire and irony of both books flow from a common source—the desire to reveal and expose reality.

In formal terms, the "life on the raft" chapter of *Huckleberry Finn* becomes very important in establishing something of a pattern in subsequent American fiction—a formal device which might be called "the pastoral touchstone chapter." Since Twain, American fiction has tended toward realism in spirit and technique. And even in our own time novelists and short story writers often feel the need to expose the basic invalidity of the transcendental ideal of a "return to nature" as the answer to the frustrating complexity of American civilization. Thoreau's exhortation to "simplify! simplify!" is devilishly attractive. Perhaps Thoreau should have added, "like Homer—*not* Theocritus." Modern man sees the return to nature as a deceptively obvious and simple solution—so obvious that even a child could see it. Or only a child.

The power of the agrarian myth and the pastoral dream has, if anything, increased since the closing of the American frontier and the pollution of Walden Pond. But that is the way classical pastoralism works: the more sophisticated and complex the Alexandrian court, the stronger the longing for the simplicity of the Arcadian Hills. The more prevalent concrete and steel, the greater the desire for grass and trees. In twentieth-century fiction and life, the farm boy has become the successful real estate salesman, the nihilistic expatriate, the legendary business mogul, the university professor, the columnist for the *New Yorker*, and the President of the United States. And he has inherited a boxed set of green-bound pastoral and agrarian values which he occasionally turns to for solutions. And, the most amazing part, he is surprised when these pastoral, agrarian, transcendental val-

ues don't work! Like Sinclair Lewis' Babbitt and John Updike's Rabbit Angstrom, he is stunned. He really is stunned
and hurt, like a child who has been tricked—like Morton's
maypolers whose idyl has been rudely and maliciously dis-
rupted. In modern politics, right-wing conservatives pastorally dream of the self-reliance of the 1840's, and lose
presidential elections. In modern fiction, we have a whole
group of characters who attempt the pastoral escape, and
inevitably fail. Often an entire short story will deal with the
pattern and theme. In the novel, this motif is often included
as a kind of aside, perhaps only a chapter or two, or even
a few important paragraphs. Thus, the "pastoral touchstone
chapter" becomes a way for the novelist to say "of course,
my hero considered the traditional American attempt to return to nature, and this is what happened."

The pattern can be shown in the works of Mark Twain,
Ernest Hemingway, and John Updike, where telling similar-
ities emerge. Briefly, the general pattern works as follows.
First, the author writes a series of stories and sketches in
which he or his characters nostalgically long for the rural
simplicity of their youth; these works include Twain's *Tom
Sawyer* and *Life on the Mississippi*; Hemingway's "Nick
Adams Stories" and the "North Woods Stories" of *In Our
Time*; and Updike's *The Same Door, Olinger Stories, Pigeon Feathers*, and *The Centaur*. Second, the author shifts
his emphasis to anti-pastoralism in which the pastoral assumptions are questioned or are used as norms for measur-
ing loss of innocence and distance from Eden. These would
include Twain's *Huckleberry Finn*, and his later pessimistic
writings; Hemingway's *A Farewell to Arms* and *The Sun
Also Rises*; and Updike's *Rabbit, Run, Of the Farm*, and
Couples. To some extent, the two groups remind us of
William Blake's *Songs of Innocence* (pastoral) and *Songs
of Experience* (anti-pastoral). In the writings of the second
group (the anti-pastorals), the heroes always make some
gesture toward returning to nature—Huck on the raft, Frederick Henry in the Alps, Jake Barnes on his trout-fishing
trip, Rabbit Angstrom as a gardener, the advertising executive on the weekend trip to his mother's farm, Piet Hanema

and "The Couples" in their very choice to live in pastoral Tarbox rather than the city. To some extent the language and imagery of the pastoral elements used in the anti-pastorals will be distinctively more lyrical and poetic than the language and imagery of the rest of the work. The pastoral elements stand out in bold relief from the rest of the work, as chapter nineteen stands out in *Huckleberry Finn.* Thus, these elements are stylistic and formal as well as thematic.

In *The Sun Also Rises,* Jake Barnes and Bill Gorton leave the city and retreat to the idyllic joy of the trout fishing trip. Atmospherically and geographically, the trip resembles a pastoral idyl, complete with "cattle grazing back in the trees," "grassy banks," rustic villages, simple food, checquered sunlight, and spring-cooled wine.[23] The fishing trip is like those Arcadian Hills in the *Idyls,* where "there was always a breeze even in the heat of the day. It was hot enough so that it felt good to wade in a cold stream, and the sun dried you when you came out and sat on the bank. We found a stream with a pool deep enough to swim in." Contrasted to the fighting bulls, searing heat, and the hellish alcoholic fog which dominate the rest of the novel, here peaceful cattle, goats, and sheep graze on the benevolent green hillside, and friends lounge on the grass and only half cynically say, "Let us rejoice in our blessings. Let us utilize the fowls of the air. Let us utilize the product of the vine. Will you utilize a little, brother?" [24] Because we are shown this idyl midway in the book, the action of the rest of the novel becomes even more nightmarish and terrifying in comparison.

In *The Great Gatsby,* Nick Carraway comes to the city with a set of essentially agrarian Midwestern values. In addition to the basic lyricism attached to Gatsby's romantic dream, other pastoral elements exist in the novel. Carraway goes through an initiation and disillusionment of the type Robin experiences in Hawthorne's "My Kinsman, Major Molineux." Much of Nick's (and Robin's) initiation involves the shattering of agrarian beliefs in human goodness and benevolence. Symbolic of Nick's innocence, he is capable of imagining a "great flock of white sheep" on Fifth Avenue. In the midst of Tom Buchanan and Myrtle Wilson's sordid affair at the "love nest," Nick innocently attempts an imaginative escape:

We drove over to Fifth Avenue, so warm and soft, almost pastoral, on the summer Sunday afternoon that I wouldn't have been surprised to see a great flock of white sheep turn the corner.[25]

The incongruity of sheep on Fifth Avenue reveals much about the tensions of Fitzgerald's novel, and his work as a whole. The Dionysian escape, the parties, adulteries, the "frisking and worse" are always doomed to failure in the American tradition. Gatsby's basic innocence is strangely akin to the innocence of Morton's maypoling pastoralists: the innocent belief that America *is* a paradise, a new Eden. Gatsby, in his desire to return to his youth when he and Daisy were swain and nymph, commits the classically tragic sin of pride. At the end of *The Great Gatsby*, this dream of paradise regained on earth is described as confronting man with "something commensurate to his capacity for wonder." And Fitzgerald suggests that this dream has been a pitfall for Americans from the time of the first explorers who gazed on the "fresh, green breast of the new world" on down to the present.[26]

The pastoral pattern can also be found in George F. Babbitt's dream of the "fairy child," in which Babbitt is a "gallant youth," and she "waited for him, in the darkness beyond mysterious groves." When finally together, Babbitt and the fairy nymph "crouched together on a shadowy hillside." [27] The dream is a version of the pastoral nymph and swain. Sinclair Lewis' *Babbitt* and John Updike's *Rabbit, Run* are alike in several ways. Both Babbitt and Rabbit find their lives mechanical and unsatisfactory; they both envision themselves as lovers; they both long for a return to nature; they both temporarily run away from "decent families." Babbitt's attempt to return to nature in the Maine woods is pathetically impotent, as is Rabbit Angstrom's stint as a gardener. Babbitt's is a dream which cannot bear the test of realization. Babbitt equates "really *living*" with being "like a trapper in a Northern Canada movie, plunging through the forest, making camp in the Rockies, a grim and wordless caveman!"

So he came to Maine, again stood on the wharf before the camp-hotel, again spat heroically into the delicate and shivering water, while the pines rustled, the mountains glowed, and a trout leaped and fell in a sliding circle.[28]

Babbitt's appeal ("like in a *movie*") is from art to life—always dangerous, and especially so in the matter of pastoralism. Like the fishing scene in *The Sun Also Rises*, the images and language are of a special sort. When Babbitt paddles out into the lake alone at night, the language becomes poetry:

The lights of the hotel and the cottages became yellow dots, a cluster of glow-worms at the base of Sachem Mountain. Larger and ever more imperturbable was the mountain in the star-filtered darkness, and the lake a limitless pavement of black marble. He was dwarfed and dumb and a little awed, but that insignificance freed him from the pomposities of being Mr. George F. Babbitt of Zenith; saddened and freed his heart.[29]

The "pastoral touchstone chapter" in *Babbitt* becomes peculiarly *anti*-pastoral when the expectations of the trip are compared with actuality. Joe Paradise, the "half-Indian and half-Yankee" guide, exists in Babbitt's mind as the ideal of the "noble savage," the free, untutored swain or frontiersman living in perfect harmony with nature. Out of shape and flabby, Joe trails behind Babbitt and pants equally. Expected by Babbitt to know the name of a "little red flower," perfectly named Joe Paradise rubs his tired back, regards the flower resentfully, and explains, "Well, some folks call it one thing and some calls it another. I always just call it Pink Flower." That ineptly pompous answer (he doesn't even say "*a* Pink Flower") is a beautiful debunking job by Lewis. Babbitt believes that Joe would like to escape even farther into the forest if he could afford it.

"Joe, what would you do if you had a lot of money? Would you stick to guiding, or would you take a claim 'way back in the woods and be independent of people?"

For the first time Joe brightened. He chewed his cud a second, and bubbled, "I've often thought of that! If I had the money, I'd go down to Tinker's Falls and open a swell shoe store." [30]

The anti-pastoral *non sequitur*. The technique is based on exactly the same premise as *As You Like It*, where the idea of the pastoral life is contrasted to the actuality. Finally, Babbitt returns to his complex, humdrum city life, and "he could not believe that he had ever been away." Joe Paradise opening a "swell shoe store" is the converse of "a flock of white sheep on Fifth Avenue," and both serve essentially the same function. The only real difference between the fishing scene in *The Sun Also Rises* and the one in *Babbitt* is that Hemingway implicitly compares the idyl to the rest of the novel, whereas Lewis explicitly exposes the pastoral myth. The function of the two scenes is essentially the same. As a matter of fact, Hemingway has his two fishermen talk about very *un*idyllic topics as they lounge on the grass: H. L. Mencken, the Scopes Trial, and Brett Ashley. The effect is similar to Joe Paradise's assertion that he'd really like to open "a swell shoe store" in town.

The patterns abound in modern literature, but time and space prohibit comment on all the examples. Certainly, the pattern directly applies to the works of John Steinbeck and William Faulkner. Consider the extent to which the pastoral and agrarian themes are treated in such works as Steinbeck's *The Grapes of Wrath, East of Eden, Of Mice and Men,* and that strangely violent idyllic failure, *To A God Unknown.* In Faulkner's work, the dichotomies between city and town, past and present, simple and sophisticated can all be related to the attitudes and assumptions of pastoral and anti-pastoral as I have treated them in this essay. Consider Faulkner's treatment of his Negro and Indian heroes and heroines, his simple, agrarian proletarians possessed with extraordinary wisdom and dignity. For example, in *The Bear* Faulkner molds his story partly to pivot on Keats's "Ode On A

Grecian Urn," which in turn focuses on the pastoral assumptions behind the paintings of the nymphs, swains, and sacrificial processionals that decorate the urn. *The Sound and the Fury*, with its symbolic golf green, and *As I Lay Dying*, with its agrarian assumptions and agrarian characters, both relate to the pattern I have described.

The works of Willa Cather almost all relate to the pastoral pattern, from *My Antonia*, with its epigraph from Virgil's *Georgics*, to those wonderful short stories like "Neighbor Rosicky," which unashamedly celebrate and mourn the pastoral ideal—much as Theocritus and Virgil celebrated and mourned it. Howard Mumford Jones, in a work of great eloquence, candor, and dignity, writes of "the frontier" in the works of Cooper, Twain, and Willa Cather. Of Willa Cather he says,

The dedication of *My Antonia* (to the daughters of a family in Red Cloud) warns the alert reader what to expect, and so does the epigraph: *Optima dies . . . prima fugit*, from Virgil's *Georgics*—the best days are the first to flee. The best days were the all too brief days of the agrarian frontier, when life was simple and heroic, before the corrupting influences of city finance, city newspapers, the city doctrine of success spoiled even the American farm—when, in sum, a spending economy took over the national mind. This contrast created the general philosophy of Miss Cather's work.[31]

Andès, near Mantua, the scene of Virgil's rural childhood, Hannibal (Twain's), upper Michigan (Hemingway's), Sauk Center (Lewis'), Red Cloud (Cather's), Shillington (Updike's)—these small lost unknown places, foreign to the tongue and unplaceable on mental maps, in the long run may have more to do with heroism and philosophy than names like Rome and Alexandria and New York and London and Chicago. Influential artists, philosophers, and thinkers—those who drive money changers from temples and ask questions of Athenian youths—often grow up in the provincial hamlets of Nazareth and Andès and Stratford, and merely do their work in Jerusalem, Athens, Rome, London, and New York. Perhaps that fact alone is a large part of what the Theocritan and Virgilian pastoral mode is all about: Arcady, Andès, Red Cloud, and Shillington may, after all, be merely pseudonyms for Eden.[32]

In conclusion, this historical survey of a pattern must be brought somewhat summarily and abruptly to a close. One could go on indefinitely—talking about Nathanael West, Glenway Wescott, Katherine Anne Porter, James Agee, Steinbeck, Bellow, Malamud, Truman Capote, Eudora Welty, Flannery O'Connor, Carson McCullers, to say nothing of the pattern in American poetry and American drama. John Barth's fantastic novel, *Giles Goat-Boy*, in which the hero is sired by a computer out of a virgin and reared as a goat, is alone a pregnant topic for an entire study in pastoral and anti-pastoral terms.

Finally, the patterns I have briefly traced—from the earliest colonial American literature, through the positive and negative romanticists, through Mark Twain and the realists, down to our own time—constitute a main current and concern in our literary history: essentially pastoral and anti-pastoral concerns. Furthermore, so far as I can discern, these are some of the most basic concerns of John Updike's fiction. I feel that the reader will better understand my following criticism of John Updike's fiction after reading this chapter. There can be no question that Updike has already established himself as a major American novelist, and anything which adds to an appreciation of his fiction is worth the trouble of both writing and reading. And for an author as conscious of his literary heritage as Updike is, failure to see his fiction in historical terms is largely a failure to see his fiction at all.

3

Primary Tensions
Eden and the Fall, Swain and Sophisticate, Farm and Town in Updike's Early Work

John Updike's first four books, *The Poorhouse Fair* (1958), *The Same Door* (1959), *Rabbit, Run* (1960), and *Pigeon Feathers* (1962), establish the clear-cut pastoral and anti-pastoral patterns which so strongly color the body of his later work. For instance, considered in sequential relation to these earlier works, the settings, characters, dramatic tensions, and existential concerns of *The Centaur* (1963) are familiar territory to the reader who has read Updike's work in sequence. Likewise, the reader of *Of the Farm* (1965) immediately perceives that he is reading a kind of sequel to *The Centaur*. After reading the works in sequence, at first one might even be annoyed by the nagging idea that Updike's work as a whole is a kind of serialized autobiography —a semifictional diary of a school teacher's sensitive young son from Shillington, Pennsylvania, who went out into the larger world to meet his fortune and fate, and who records his yearly progress from hopeful adolescence to harried young fatherhood to middle-aged sophistication with studied stylistic attention to lyricism, detail and "the phrase and carriage of everyday life." Confirmed in his diagnosis by outright autobiography like Updike's "The Dogwood Tree: A Boyhood," the skeptic might pass John Updike off as a gifted craftsman of slick autobiographical prose. Should he arrive at this conclusion, he would have missed the point of Updike's fiction. *Of the Farm* is a sequel to *Pigeon Feathers* and *The Centaur*—somewhat in the way that *Huckleberry Finn* is a "sequel" to *Tom Sawyer*. The works can be seen as part of a pattern. The continuity and reappearance of characters and settings in Updike's work is "autobiographical" and "sequential" much in the way that William Faulkner's "Yoknapatawpha County" is contiguous within Faulkner's work, or, to exaggerate the point, in the way Odysseus keeps reappearing within *The Odyssey*. In short, patterns and themes exist within Updike's or any artist's work as surely as they exist in experience itself—patterns as basic as seasons, diurnal rotations, pulses, the physicist's rhythms. Of these rhythms and patterns in Updike's work, pastoral and anti-pastoral themes occur as regularly as, say, those sunflooding windows opening into Vermeer's cool, shadowed interiors. And like the subtle tensions between Vermeer's lights and darks—tensions and complexities which fascinate Updike's own painter's eye, incidentally—the variations between pastoral and anti-pastoral patterns in Updike's fiction provide a rich subject for study, and a fertile record of some fundamentally shared experiences of American intellectuals in our time.

The Poorhouse Fair, The Same Door, and *Pigeon Feathers and Other Stories* should be considered as a group. They are essentially works about the effects of agrarian values on very old people and very young people. It is in these works that the primary tensions between farm and town, past and present, simplicity and sophistication are articulated. The stories often pit pastoralism against anti-pastoralism in a dogged debate; insofar as small-town simplicity is treated nostalgically, and boyhood innocence is treated lyrically, pastoralism wins. The teen-age hero is a type of swain—poor, sensitive, perceptive, intelligent, rather femininely poetic. Often the boy's father is a realistic intellectual, a scientist, a moralist, a sophisticate. But, insofar as that simplicity and innocence are quietly but insistently questioned, contradicted, and undermined throughout the stories, anti-pastoralism lurks in the background as a powerful, potentially satiric force. As Edward William Taylor has said, the satiric reflex is "built in." I propose, then, that John Updike tends to work somewhat from the position of the longing, celebratory, nostalgic pastoralist in his early works toward the position of the cynical, satiric, militant anti-pastoralist in his more recent works. Indeed, it is one of these relatively early works, *Rabbit, Run*, which arises as one of the definitive anti-pastoral, anti-transcendental works in modern literature. Because *Rabbit, Run* is so significant to the anti-pastoral pattern, I will deal with it in a separate chapter. Meanwhile, I will examine some of the primary patterns in *The Poorhouse Fair*, *The Same Door*, and *Pigeon Feathers and Other Stories*.

In several ways, the idyllic and nostalgic tones and themes of Updike's early works correspond to the tones and themes of Mark Twain's early works. Furthermore, Updike's early emphasis on youth and innocence have both natural sequence and historical precedent: as *Tom Sawyer* precedes *Huckleberry Finn*, youth precedes maturity, Eden precedes the expulsion, Emersonian transcendentalism precedes twentieth-century cybernetic values. In Updike's work, experiences set in pastoral Olinger serve as prerequisites and foils to sophisticated New York experiences as surely as experimental, exploratory adolescent sexuality serves as a prerequisite to the free-wheeling fornication of the Tarbox "Couples."

In "The Dogwood Tree: A Boyhood," John Updike explains that the "Three Great Secret Things" of his youth were 1) Religion, 2) Sex, and 3) Art.[1] They have remained the great themes of Updike's work, and they are curiously related to pastoral and anti-pastoral patterns in his fiction. First, religion. Two works, *The Poorhouse Fair* and the title story of *Pigeon Feathers and Other Stories*, reveal telling relationships between religion and attitudes toward the earth and nature. The hero of *The Poorhouse Fair* is ninety-four years old, and lives at the county Poor Farm; the hero of "Pigeon Feathers" is fourteen years old, and lives on his grandparents' unmodernized farm outside of Olinger. Aged ninety-four and aged fourteen, both heroes are confronted with challenges to their religious faith, and both heroes struggle to affirm that faith—the aged Hook in his debate with Conner, the adolescent David in his debate with Reverend Dobson. The modes of confrontation and affirmation are related to the assumptions which in the previous chapter I suggested were basically versions of pastoral.

An important fact about these two stories is that both occur on farms—isolated agrarian islands in an ocean of mid-twentieth-century technology and supercivilization. This motif—the isolated, anachronistic farm setting or rural village setting—is central to Updike's fiction. It occurs in all the short stories set in Olinger or its variously named equivalent small towns or villages; furthermore, Updike often removes his pastoral settings to even greater extremes by locating his stories on farms and in woods and fields outside of the small town. This movement from city to small country town to primitive farmhouse is a type of reverse telescoping which dramatically defines the pattern. It suggests movement in time as well as in space. Turning from the superhighway to the macadam road to the dirt lane is a recurrent symbol in Updike's fiction. In *The Poorhouse Fair*, the Poor Farm "lorded over a considerable agricultural plain in New Jersey," and its four-and-a-half acres were enclosed by a high stone wall. It is isolated from even the nearest village. So is the Pennsylvania farm setting of "Pigeon Feathers." So is the Caldwell farm home in *The Centaur*, and in *Of the Farm*. In *Couples*, Tarbox is a pastoral village physically isolated from Boston, with a village green at its center. This characteristic setting, from the first novel through *Couples*, is perhaps the strongest evidence and clue for seeing Updike's work in terms of pastoral and anti-pastoral patterns. The settings are as symbolic and integral to theme as the Arcadian Hills and Slopes of Hybla are to Theocritus' work—or Walden Pond and the Mississippi River are to Thoreau's and Twain's.

The Poorhouse Fair confronts the reader with two religious alternatives—alternatives which become crystallized in the ideological confrontation between Mr. Hook, the nonagenarian ex-school-teacher, and Conner, the young Utopian Socialist director of the Poor Farm. The theological alternatives polarize at the ideas of Eden before the Fall and Eden after the Fall. Hook clings unshakably to traditional Christian orthodox faith; Conner just as religiously believes in "Heaven placed on this earth" through the imposition of science and man's willed control of his environment. The dream reminds us of Utopia, Eden, Arcadia, Merry Mount, and the Blessed Isles; the Utopian Poor Farm echoes its American predecessor, Brook Farm. By a strange reversal, Conner's Utopian concepts relate to the pastoral attitude, despite the fact that Conner's dream world of the future will ironically be composed of steel and glass and atomic reactors; his Edenic Poor Farm of the future (the idyllic totalitarian state) is curiously like the transcendentalists' Brook Farm of the past: they both exist in the mind as ideals and are both ultimately contradicted by empirical reality and human nature. All the action of *The Poorhouse Fair*, like the action of *The Blithedale Romance*, negates the possibility of the realization of the ideal.

Conner describes his concept of Heaven on Earth, which he equates with the abolition of all pain, and therefore all evil. It is the dream of Eden before the Fall. It is the totalitarian state of the future. And with its "conserved rivers," the "beauty of the landscape," "work and love, parks, and orchards," it is strikingly similar to Thomas Morton's "New English Canaan" and Crèvecoeur's description of America in his *Letters from a New England Farmer*. Conner says,

Money too may have vanished. The state will receive what is made and give what is needed. Imagine this continent—the great cities things of beauty; squalor gone; the rivers conserved; the beauty of the landscape, conserved. No longer suffering but beauty will be worshipped. Art will mirror no longer struggle but fulfillment. Each man will know himself—without delusions, without muddle, and within the limits of that self-knowledge will construct a sane and useful life. Work and love: parks, orchards. Understand me. The factors which for ages have warped the mind of man will grow like a tree in the open. There will be no waste. No pain and above all no waste. And this heaven *will* come to *this* earth, and come soon.[2]

An old woman listening to this idyl sardonically interpolates the vision, "Naked girls on the seashore." The reply is suggestive enough that Conner later envisions his Golden Age of the future in terms reminiscent of Greek swains and nymphs.

Hook's response to Conner's challenge of his faith is the

traditional Christian resonse: Faith is irrational; God is unknowable; the visible universe manifests a divine creator; pain and suffering provide the opportunity for the exercise of virtue. Like all faith, it is somewhat desperate, as well as consolatory. Hook, benign, gentle, intellectual, is "transcendental" only to the extent that he sees physical nature as emblematic of spiritual realities; after that, he proceeds by irrational faith.

But it is not Hook's words which finally win the argument. Rather, it is the actions of the old people as a group. Later that same day, while picking up stones from a wrecked portion of fence, the indigent old inmates of the home spontaneously begin to stone the young Utopian dreamer. It is the classic communal sin. And evil, sin, and death—those timeless spoilers of Edens and Utopias and idyls—invade the grounds of the Poor Farm. Hook, the only innocent among the group of stoners, is unjustly punished by Conner. Conner insists on asserting to himself that "Man is good," even in the face of contradictory evidence and behavior which says, "Man is fallen; we are all sinners." In refusing Conner's suggestion that she move her fair exhibit to a cool shade, an old woman explains to him, "We're too old and too mean; we're too tired." [3] She might as well be speaking for the race, which has grown "old and mean" since the eating of the forbidden fruit. Having set their spiritual stalls in the sun through disobedience to God, men can merely dream of shadowy groves and create them in idyllic art.

Thus, there is something basically anti-pastoral about the old people at the Poor Farm—rather in the way the Plymouth Puritans were anti-pastoral in their refusal to believe in "Heaven on earth." The young reformer in *The Poorhouse Fair* is portrayed as effete, sentimental, and vainly proud, although he sees himself as a messianic figure. The novel—set in the future ("less than a year away from the Crystal anniversary of the St. Lawrence Seaway")—is as unlikely a first novel as has been written by a modern American. Written at age twenty-six, the novel reveals a remarkable insight into age, faith, the human condition. Conservative only in its celebration of freedom, dignity, and spontaneity, the novel pleads only for the conservation of those values worth conserving: a wildness of spirit, and the integrity of inviolable individuality. Utopias, Edens, idyls seem tame and dull in comparison to sinful man hoping and working for the redemption of his individual soul, confronting the terrible mystery of faith. Much of the terror of the novel stems from the fact that Conners (well-meaning con men?) have already attained power; and the proud doctrine of "manifest destiny" seems (at least on the surface) more powerful than the doctrine of sin and salvation.

One of the primary conflicts in *The Poorhouse Fair* is based on the clashing character traits and philosophies of Conner, the new director, and Mendelssohn, the former director. Mendelssohn had been a daytime drinker, a lazy, supercilious administrator, and a physically unattractive despot. He had ruled the old poeple with an iron hand, and he had refused to socialize with them or even to eat at the same table with them: "Mendelssohn had in part thought of himself as God." And the old people had loved and respected him. Conner, the sentimental Utopian socialist, "thought of no one as God." Obviously, Mendelssohn is like the authoritarian God of Puritanism—aloof, distant, unbending, but commanding respect. In contrast, Conner's transcendental humanism is flaccid and watery, and the old people know it. Significantly, the inmates of the Poor Farm had more freedom under Mendelssohn than they have under Conner. Mendelssohn realized that heaven could not be achieved on earth; both he and his wise subjects refused to dream the pastoral dream of a return to Eden.

In "Pigeon Feathers" the relationship between the "Great Secret Thing," Religion, and pastoralism is more sharply defined than in *The Poorhouse Fair*. In *The Poorhouse Fair*, the pastoral pattern works largely by extension of the implications of a general attitude. In "Pigeon Feathers," the connections are explicit and dominant. The family has just moved from the small town of Olinger to the old family farm out in the country. The religious crisis of the adolescent boy is significantly placed against the backdrop of this shift back into an agrarian environment. The boy's mother and father, both well-educated people, carry on a dialogue in the background—a continuing debate about the virtues of "organic farming," as opposed to "chemical farming." The mother's position is the pastoralist's, with her assertion that the soil has a soul, and that farming is the most honorable of the professions. The father, a chemistry teacher, "was frightened of the farm and seized any excuse to get away"; he is the anti-pastoralist.

David's religious crisis arises when he reads H. G. Well's *The Outline of History*. The rationalistic historian explains Jesus as "an obscure political agitator, a kind of hobo, in a minor colony of the Roman Empire." [4] When the boy questions his Lutheran clergyman about an afterlife, the Reverend Mr. Dobson explains that it is "like Lincoln's goodness living after him." The young clergyman is essentially a liberal transcendentalist, and his response serves only to confuse the boy further. Caught in a vacuum of doubt, the boy searches for answers. His father is the orthodox Christian in the family. On Sunday mornings he goes to church, while the mother roams the fields, occasionally accompanied by her son. Like most of Updike's women, the mother is associated with the archetypal pattern of the "earth mother." The father, in contrast, is associated with mind and spirit (as teacher and believer). These polarities which associate women with earth and matter, and men with mind and spirit exist throughout Updike's fiction; marriage and sexual union are symbolic of "the marriage of earth and heaven," the reconciliation of warring pastoralism and anti-pastoralism. Furthermore, the mother idealizes farm life in the traditional pastoral way: despite the unproductivity of the land, the inconveniences of outdoor toilets, inadequate water supplies, and the distance from employment, she insists on seeing rural life as beautiful, rich, and good. This is the Theocritan attitude and the Virgilian moral distinction.

Also, a city boy by birth, [the father] was frightened of the farm and seized any excuse to get away. The farm had been David's mother's birthplace; it had been her idea to buy it back. With an ingenuity and persistence unparalleled in her life, she had gained that end, and moved them all here—her son, her husband, her mother. . . . Strange, out in the country, amid eighty acres, they were crowded together. His father expressed his feelings of discomfort by conducting with Mother an endless argument about organic farming. All through dusk, all through supper, it rattled on.[5]

In contrast to the mother's persistent pastoral orientation, the boy and the father sought escape from the farm. The mother, in her love of the land, is aligned with the traditional dream of "Eden before the Fall," when man and nature were in harmony. The father, with his chemistic reasoning, his urban orientation, and his conventional faith, is somewhat closer to the orthodox tradition.

The question of David's faith and his fear of death is resolved through a strange union of 1) an act of killing, and 2) a subsequent transcendental insight into the unity of the universe. He is assigned the task of killing pigeons in the old barn where unused furniture is stored. With a rifle, he pumps bullets into the pigeons as they flee through a small round hole high in the barn wall. The rifle, the hole, the boy's age all have Freudian connotations. But more important is the sensation of pleasure derived from the violent act of killing: "He felt like a beautiful avenger." "He had the sensation of a creator." [6] Like the violent act of the stoning in *The Poorhouse Fair*, the violent act of shooting the pigeons unites the boy with death, sin, evil—initiating him into "the Order of Sinners," the race. Like the pastoral hero's initiation in Hawthorne's "My Kinsman, Major Molineux," David's destructive act paradoxically becomes salvational. The paradox is essentially part of the Hebraic-Christian tradition associated with concepts such as "the fortunate Fall," death as a prerequisite for life, and loss as a prerequisite for gain. Having created death through the act of shooting, the boy achieves transcendental insight through contemplation of his kill. Significantly, his mother rather than his father arrives to help him bury the birds. They choose a plot of ground "too steep to plant and mow" where "wild strawberries grew in the tangled grass." The mother, the pre-lapsarian pastoralist, makes the boy bury the birds alone: "While he went to the tool shed for the shovel, she went into the house. Unlike her, she did not look up, either at the orchard to the right of her or at the meadow on her left, but instead held her head rigidly, tilted a little, as if listening to the ground." [7] In the face of death (the slain pigeons are like the slain deer in Shakespeare's Arden Forest), the pastoralist must face very real anti-pastoral facts of life. The mother's orchards and meadows have been penetrated by sin, evil, and death. In minutely examining the "geometrical tides" of the feathers, the boy feels that the patterns and rhythms seem to have been "executed in a controlled rapture." In death the birds become beautiful; in their beauty, they become life-affirming and salvational.

As he fitted the last two, still pliant, on the top, and stood up, crusty coverings were lifted from him, and with a feminine, slipping sensation along his nerves that seemed to give the air hands, he was robed in this certainty: that the God who had lavished such craft upon these worthless birds would not destroy His Whole Creation by refusing to let David live forever.[8]

The conclusion of the story would be little more than an Emersonian transcendental insight, were it not for the destructive impetus behind the intuitive "certainty," and were it not for the essential element of paradox. The lyricism of the final passage of "Pigeon Feathers" does celebrate the beauty of nature. But it is far closer to a pastoral lament than to anything else: for example, in the way that Milton transforms Lycidas's seemingly senseless death into an affirmation of afterlife, Updike transforms the seemingly senseless act of killing into an affirmation. And in the way that "Lycidas" is a combination of Greek pastoral and Christian orthodoxy, "Pigeon Feathers" is a combination of negative and positive American transcendentalism. Like the lyricism at the end of Herman Melville's Billy Budd, the lyricism at the end of "Pigeon Feathers" arrives only after a series of physically violent and spiritually anguished incidents. Like Hawthorne and Melville, rather than Emerson, Updike avoids the easy pastoral answers to questions of faith and belief. Still, insight, affirmation, and lyricism characterize Updike's early treatments of "the First Great Secret Thing." This thematic and stylistic positivism exists because Updike's early work leans toward being a version of serious pastoralism. The lyricism tends to be ironic in his later works. In the totality of his work, such religious affirmation is associated only with the very young, the very old, and the very naïve. Characters "robed in certainty" become increasingly fewer as his work progresses. In *The Centaur* and *Of the Farm*, we see this same boy and his parents again— grown older and even more removed from Eden. John Updike's characters "have all sinned, and fallen short of the Glory of God" (Rom. 3:23).

Along with religion, sex is another of Updike's "Great Secret Things," and sexual lyricism nostalgically haunts his early short stories set in Olinger. In his foreword to *Olinger Stories: A Selection* (Vintage, 1964), John Updike establishes the setting of his early works as a pastoral enchanted world of "rural memories, accents, and superstitions." [9] The setting of the Olinger stories (the name is pronounced, according to Updike, "with a long *O*, a hard *g*") is, like the setting of the prototypic pastoral idyls, "a state of mind, of my mind, and belongs entirely to me." [10] The stories collected in *Olinger Stories* were originally published in book form in the collections *The Same Door* and *Pigeon Feathers and Other Stories*. But, more significant to the overall tradition of pastoral literature, the stories were all published first of all in the *New Yorker* magazine. They conform to the pattern of the sophisticated Theocritus writing pastoral, semiautobiographical, rural fiction for the fashionable Alexandrian courtiers. Updike describes the setting of his stories as follows:

Olinger is west of greater Philadelphia and south of the coal regions and contains a box factory and a small hosiery mill which in World War II made parachutes. Most of its citizens look economically toward Alton, a middle-sized city whose industries are steel, textiles, pretzels, and beer. The surrounding land is loamy, and Olinger is haunted—hexed, perhaps—by rural memories, accents, and superstitions. Cars traveling through see nothing here to make them stop; the town is neither young nor old, poor nor rich, backward nor forward. It is beyond the western edge of Megalopolis, and hangs between its shallow hills enchanted, nowhere, anywhere; there is no place like it.[11]

The heroes of the stories are "at bottom the same boy, a local boy." Of the relation of the stories to his own life, Updike explains, "Not an autobiography, they have made one impossible." Further explaining the order of the stories in the collection, Updike comments on the hero:

They have been arranged here in the order of the hero's age; in the beginning he is ten, in the middle stories he is an adolescent, in the end he has reached manhood. He wears different names and his circumstances vary, but he is at bottom the same boy, a local boy—this selection could be called A Local Boy. The locality is that of Olinger, Pennsylvania, a small town bounded on the urban side by Alton and on the rural side by Firetown.[12]

This hero is a version of the prototypic pastoral swain, himself a "local boy" in the vicinity of Mount Hybla or Arcady.

Several of the stories in this group can be seen as types of pastoral love lyrics, in which the young swain enjoys types of innocent sexual awakenings while "sporting with Naerea [or Molly Bingaman or Mary Landis] in the shade." The beautiful and often painful idyllic lyricism of these early stories of sexual awakenings is especially important in the overall scope of Updike's work, because later the attempts of characters like Rabbit Angstrom and Piet Hanema to recapture that adolescent lyricism become sources of pain, anguish, and destruction. In Updike's more recent work, the pastoral love lyric has become a harshly ironic anti-pastoral touchstone.

In what he calls a "barefaced reminiscence" (i.e., "The Dogwood Tree: A Boyhood," published in Assorted Prose), Updike explains how sex and nature were related in his mind from the time of his early childhood. When he was a child, his parents took him on nature walks into the woods, as if they wanted him to learn and feel some relation to nature and the earth. He did not learn it until he was sexually mature.

This broad crescent of woods is threaded with our walks and suffused with images of love. For it was here, on the beds of needles under the canopies of low pine boughs, that our girls— and this is later, not boyhood at all, but the two have become entangled—were rumored to give themselves. Indeed, I was told that one of the girls in our class, when we were in the ninth grade, had boasted that she liked nothing so much as skinny-dipping in the dam and then making love under the pines. As for myself, this was beyond me, and may be myth, but I do remember, when I was seventeen, taking a girl on one of those walks from my childhood so (then) long ago. We had moved from town, but only ten miles, and my father and I drove in to the high school every day. We walked, the girl and I, down the path where I had smashed so many branches, and sat down on a damp broad log—it was early spring, chilly, a timid froth of leaves overhead—and I dared lightly embrace her from behind and cup my hands over her breasts, small and shallow within the stiffness of her coat, and she closed her eyes and tipped her head back, and an adequate apology seemed delivered for the irritable innocence of these almost forgotten hikes with my parents.[13]

This reminiscence reminds us of another of Updike's scenes where lovers not only caress, but also copulate orally and genitally "on a bed of needles under canopies of low pine boughs"—when the middle-aged adulterers Piet Hanema and Georgene Thorne make love on the pine-strewn sun-roof in *Couples*. In the genuinely lyrical Olinger stories, the idea of swain and nymph making love and discovering sex in a natural setting is idyllically charming and pastorally refreshing; in *Couples* the idea has become jadedly sordid and a little ridiculous. Speaking of a quarry near "the tougher section," of Shillington (Olinger), Updike says, "The legends of love that scattered condoms along its grassy edges seemed to be of a coarser love than that which perfumed the woods." [14] Updike's older antiheroes long for love "that perfumed the woods"—that is, the love of nymphs and swains in a pastoral grove. The sexual language of the early and later works reveals the basic shift in attitude: for example, in Olinger, for a girl to fall trustfully asleep beside the adolescent swain makes him "The Happiest [He's]

Been"; in Tarbox, the act and the language of "love" have been reduced to pornographic parodic maxims like "To fuck is human; to be blown, divine." [15] And the concomitant contrasting lyricism in the later works has become essentially ironic.

In his foreword to the selection of *Olinger Stories*, Updike comments on the timelessness of that "local boy" who keeps reappearing in the stories:

It surprised me, in making this arrangement, to realize that the boy who wrestles with H. G. Wells and murders pigeons is younger than the one who tells Thelma Lutz she shouldn't pluck her eyebrows. But we age unevenly, more slowly in society than in our own skulls.[16]

Of course the hero is timeless, partly because he is as old as the first Theocritan pastoral swain who sang love lyrics on the slopes of the Arcadian Hills, and as young as all adolescents have always been since the beginning of the race.

"Friends from Philadelphia" was the first piece of fiction John Updike ever sold, and it curiously conforms to a dichotomous pattern of conflict between the pastoral swain and the anti-pastoral sophisticate. It conforms in several ways. First, the story is about a fifteen-year-old boy who has come from the farm into the small town of Olinger to buy a bottle of inexpensive wine because his parents are expecting to entertain old college friends from the city; furthermore, the story was sold to, and first published in the *New Yorker*, the American epitome of urbane sophistication. In both subject matter (the poor, sensitive, perceptive rural boy shyly and indirectly wooing the young nymph) and attitude (the Theocritan assumption that a sophisticated courtly audience will be interested in the unsophisticated amours of the simple swain), the story fits into the pastoral pattern.

Details within the story itself conform to the pattern. In a touch of ironic fictional "screw-turning," rural John Nordholm seeks the aid of an only *relatively urban* small-town family in buying the wine. The daughter, Thelma Lutz, having visited New York, "tried to talk the way she thought they talked there," and she plucks her eyebrows. The mother sees herself as a liberal sophisticate because she allows Thelma to "smoke right in her own home, her own living room, if she wants to." And the drunken father tastelessly flaunts the fact that he, although uneducated, buys a new car every year, while John's college-educated father drives an old Plymouth. Mr. Lutz goes into the liquor store and buys a bottle of expensive imported vintage wine for the boy, and pretends it is cheap domestic wine. Economically superior only, the Lutz family have acquired material wealth, and have affected sophisticated airs. But in the story, they are shown to be pretentiously absurd, and nothing else. Conforming to the pastoral pattern, the Nordholms are poorer but nobler, less pretentious, but more perceptive than the town family.

The story is also vaguely and subtly sexual. A kind of literary defloration and thematic prediction of things to come, the first sentence of the first story John Updike ever sold shows an adolescent swain stealing a glimpse of an adolescent nymph's thigh:

In the moment before the door was opened to him, he glimpsed her thigh below the half-drawn shade. Thelma was home, then. She was wearing the Camp Winniwoho T shirt and her quite short shorts.[17]

The innocence of this adolescent sexuality suggests the innocence and simplicity of sexuality in the Theocritan *Idyls*. Especially in contrast to the role of sex in later works like *Rabbit, Run* and *Couples* (where sexual promiscuity and sexual excesses become associated with drowned babies and abortions), the faltering sexual awakenings in these early stories can only be described as genuinely idyllic. In "Friends from Philadelphia," the swain makes his subtly sexual assault on the nymph—verbally—by telling Thelma Lutz, "Don't pluck your eyebrows." And from the sheer pride of asserting his maleness, John gives her the advice twice.

John Updike has also pointed out that in two of the

Olinger stories, "Flight" and "A Sense of Shelter," the young boy pursues unattainable young girls, Molly Bingaman and Mary Landis. Updike suggests that the rural orientation and home of the boy has something to do with the fact that he does not win the girls. In the nonfiction foreword to *Olinger Stories* Updike says,

In fact, my family moved ten miles away from the town when I was thirteen. . . . This strange distance, this less than total remove from my milieu, is for all I know the crucial detachment of my life. In some stories, like "Flight" and "A Sense of Shelter," I have pretended the physical distance did not exist, but it is there, as the enchantment that makes Molly Bingaman and Mary Landis unattainable.[18]

Updike explains his removal to the farm as possibly "the crucial detachment" of his life. Perhaps it is also the crucial detachment of his fiction from mere "Howellsian Realism" or "slick *New Yorker* sketches." Updike is working in terms of a broadly conceived pastoral myth or fable. And much of his detachment and worth as an artist is integrally related to the "crucial" pastoral and anti-pastoral patterns which run through his life and his fiction. An "enchantment" does make Molly Bingaman and Mary Landis unattainable. It is partly the hero's distance in time and space, and partly the enchantment of art: on Grecian urns and in pastoral fiction, the "fair youth" never "has his bliss"; both he and the maidens are enchanted, frozen in time and space. Molly Bingaman and Mary Landis cannot fade, because their eternal youth and fairness have been sculpted on the idyllic curves of John Updike's rather urnlike pastoral short stories. In his later fiction, his antiheroes—unable to distinguish between the past and the present, the ideal and the real, art and life, enchantments and hexes—embark on disastrous sexual quests for these fair maidens. In *Couples*, Piet Hanema's Annabelle Vojt is merely another name for Molly Bingaman and Mary Landis.

In stories like "The Persistence of Desire," the ex-swain—now a married man with two children—may return to Olinger to have his eyes checked by an oculist, and accidentally run into one of the Olinger nymphs, also married.

He may try to arrange an adulterous tryst; but it won't quite be the same. In real life, nymphs do marry, fade, and age; swains grow bald, paunchy, and nearsighted. Updike's antiheroes psychologically share the plea, "O! Let us linger in Eden."

The "Great Secret Thing" of sex becomes increasingly important in Updike's fiction—on through to the orgiastic eroticism and ironic lyricism of *Couples*. But the legitimate lyricism of those sexual awakenings in the Olinger stories becomes correspondingly important, as a norm and a touchstone. Characters who try to return to those lost adolescent ecstasies usually ruin themselves and others in the attempt. As Updike has said, Olinger "hangs between its shallow hills enchanted, nowhere, anywhere; there is no place like it." Therefore, you can't get back there except through the mind and imagination. The reader who mistakenly passes these early Olinger stories off as merely skillful sketches has a serious problem: he has either forgotten his own personal Olinger, or he is not equipped to respond to the aesthetics of authentic Grecian urns—or Keatsian odes—or Virgilian *Eclogues*—and that is a great pity.

Updike's third "Great Secret Thing" is art; and in his early works Updike tends to associate art, artists, and craftmanship with the "Golden Age." To the extent that craftsmanship is shown in his fiction as a thing of the past, it is a significant part of the loss which Updike mourns throughout his work. Consequently, it becomes associated with the lost pastoral ideal, which also includes innocent sexuality and naïve religious faith.

From his first novel, *The Poorhouse Fair* (1958), through *Couples* (1968), Updike has included characters and details which celebrate the simple, faithful craftsman as a kind of minor hero. For example, in the early work, *The Poorhouse Fair*, this figure is represented by an old woman who creates patchwork quilts, and an old man who carves peach seeds into tiny charms. In *Couples*, the "venerable carpenters," Adams and Comeau, represent a type of Golden Age of Carpentry in their attention to detail and craftsmanship. The quilt-maker, the charm-carver, the master finish-carpenter are all versions of anachronistic rustic artisans, superannuated and headed toward extinction. In Updike's fiction these artist-craftsmen are consistently foiled by mass-production techniques and dehumanizing mechanization.

Two of John Updike's prose essays shed light on this motif: "Old and Precious," a critique of an antique show, and "Grandma Moses," a critique of the pastorally oriented primitive painter.[19] "Old and Precious," an urbane review for the *New Yorker*, begins in satire of antique-hounds, and ends in ambiguity: "On the way out, we experimentally opened what we took to be a fancy toothpick holder. Inside, there was a miniature button-hook for a baby's shoes. How precious. How old." [20] But the main tone of the essay is that past ages did include something of value—something now lost and untenable. Consider the implications of the comments on "primitivism" versus "sophistication":

Speaking of feet, there was the Joseph Burger collection of footwear, which proved that the poorer the wearer, the more sensible the shoe. The Mexican peasant's leather sandals, the Chinese coolie's "bird's-nest" boots, and the Norwegian yeoman's woven shoes set a norm of comfort and simplicity from which sophistication could only depart, tweaking the toes upward (Turkey and Syria), adding square flaps to the front (Bohemia), piling on width (dunderbludgeons, popular under Henry VIII), adding height (Japanese clogs), and, in a frenzy of civilization, withering the foot itself into a pitiful flipper that could fit into a five-inch envelope of flowered cloth (China).[21]

The peasantry "*set a norm of comfort and simplicity from which sophistication could only depart.*" The comment comprises a type of manifesto when seen in relation to the pastoral tradition, and when taken in connection with the entire body of John Updike's fiction. Early stories like "The Blessed Man of Boston, My Grandmother's Thimble, and Fanning Island" pick up these assumptions and celebrate the pastoral "norm of comfort and simplicity." The important point about "Old and Precious" is that Updike is torn between satire and eulogy in the essay—as he is torn between the values of pastoral Shillington and anti-pastoral New York.

The short eulogy of Mrs. Moses and her pastoral paintings also ties in with the third "Great Secret Thing." Here
Updike celebrates the primitive artist as being like "old
buildings in a city" or "church spires in a landscape"—that
is, *civilizing* influences that "make the world seem safer."
Grandma Moses, who once said, "I paint from the top
down. First the sky, then the mountains, then the hills,
then the houses, then the cattle, and then the people," [22]
becomes aligned with Amy Mortis, the old quilt-maker of
The Poorhouse Fair, who ranged the pattern of her quilt
from a scene of flowers, rivers, blue sky, and Palladian temples (classical pastoral simplicity), down to the savage reds
and golds and greens of the earth (the real world). [23]
Strangely like aged Mrs. Moses and Amy Mortis, young Mr.
Updike paints from the lyrical pastoralism of reminiscence
down to the fallen corruption of sophisticated reality—from
heaven to earth, from idyl to its parody the suburb, from
Arcady to Alexandria, from Shillington to New York, and
(with consummate irony) from Olinger to Tarbox.

Not only does Updike celebrate and mourn the simple
craftsman and artisan in his work, but he also associates
more sophisticated art with the young adolescent, the "local
boy" of the Olinger stories. Variously, the young hero of the
early stories is often a version of either a scholar-theologian
(as in "Pigeon Feathers," "Dentistry and Doubt," and
"Lifeguard"), or some type of artist (as in "Ace in the
Hole," "Still Life," and "A Sense of Shelter"). He is the
heroic swain, Peter-Prometheus, of *The Centaur*, youthfully
obsessed with Vermeer's clarity of theme and execution:
the aspiring young artist who winds up later doing illustra-
tive hackwork, or painting nonobjective abstract failures,
"vast canvasses—so oddly expensive as raw materials, so
oddly worthless transmuted into art." [24] Or, later still, he is
Piet Hanema of *Couples*, forced to mass produce flimsy
ranch houses rather than restore dignified old colonial
homes.

Art is associated with the pastoral idyl early in Updike's
work—even before the clear associations in *The Centaur*.
The museum on the outskirts of Alton is associated with

fountains and black swans and nature lessons in the basement. In "Still Life," the young art students also go down into the basement to "draw from nature." In "Packed Dirt, Churchgoing, A Dying Cat, A Traded Car," the museum appears as a cultural island, "where every tree and flowerbed wore a name-tag and black swans drifted through flotillas of crumbled bread." [25] Upstairs there were "slashed paintings of Pennsylvania woodland by the Shearers and bronze statuettes of wrestling Indians that stirred my first erotic dreams."

and, in the round skylit room at the head of the marble stairs, a black-rimmed pool in whose center a naked green lady held to her pursed lips a shell whose lucent contents forever spilled from the other side, filling this whole vast upstairs—from whose Palladian windows the swans in their bready pond could be seen trailing fan-shaped wakes—with the music and chill romance of falling water.[26]

This museum with its falling water, swans, sculpture, and serenity is a recurrent symbol which joins idealized nature and idealized art in Updike's fiction. This association of art and nature, the created ideal and the natural ideal (cool, sculpted naked green ladies and real black swans) is a part of the pattern of pastoralism in Updike's own fictional art—the swan-circled island of pastoral reminiscence as contrasted to the condom-strewn "tougher side of town." Both are present in his work. The swans keep reappearing, but in the later works they are ironic, like the DC–3, a "swan boat mildly bobbing," in "The Wait." And in contrast to the cold, sculpted elegance of that "naked green lady" with the shell, the "ladies" of *Couples* are noteworthily hot and fleshy.

Thus, in two ways art and artists become associated with pastoralism in the early works: 1) simple folk arts and crafts, and 2) the adolescent swain's dream of becoming a fine artist. In a way, Updike's own fictional reminiscences can be seen as pastorals written in the Theocritan tradition. To this extent, he is a highly sophisticated artist; furthermore, to see the early works as pastorals explains Updike's employment of lyricism in the greater scheme of his works.

Those critics who would pass these early works off as insignificant are the same ones who would pass the pastoral mode itself off as insignificant. As C. S. Lewis has said, and as John Updike knows, the pastoral is "a region in the mind which does exist and which should be visited often." [27]

In the light of John Updike's later anti-pastoral works, the early stories become even more important, and more a coherent part of a thematic and stylistic pattern—a whole and a totality which, if not tragic, is at least meaningfully melancholic in the way that wisdom itself is melancholy. For a writer such as Theocritus to remind us of those far-off lost Slopes of Arcady is alone a painful assault on the sensibility; for a writer like Shakespeare to remind us that the slopes were never really that perfect and pleasant to begin with pushes painful loss toward tragic negation. Updike does both—seriously reminds us of lyrical pastoral tranquility in the early works, and then continues to employ the reminder as an ironic and satirical norm in the later works. The result is a double-edged knife which Updike keeps twisting, like some old colonial Calvinist enduring the spiritual torture of knowing the inexorable reality of both God's mercy and God's wrath—and finding peace in neither.

4

Rabbit, Run
An Anti-Pastoral Satire

An *angstrom* is one ten-billionth of a meter. Harry ("Rabbit") Angstrom, the hero of *Rabbit, Run*, is blatantly christened by Updike, and turned loose in the novel to run and drive in circles, finger the "lettuce" in his wallet, sleep in the windowed "hutch" of his car, impregnate two women, become a gardener, and run off into the woods at the end. His wife Janet is a "Springer"; his old coach Tothero is a "Tot-hero"; his Lutheran minister Kruppenbach is a "horses's backside." [1] Is something satirical and allegorical going on behind this wild punning? One might not gather so from reading much of the major published criticism on *Rabbit, Run*—mainly criticism which somberly analyzes Rabbit Angstrom as a bleak Sartrian existentialist and post-Nietzschian seeker, a kind of ignorant but inspired folk-philosopher.[2] Are we to accept these name-puns and exaggerated details as whimsical linguistic indulgences within a highly serious realistic novel about the tragic paradoxes involved in the novel's epigraph: "The motions of Grace, the hardness of the heart; external circumstances?" [3] The name-tags are insignificant only if we accept names such as "Arden," "Touchstone," "Sir Oliver Martext," "Silvius," and "Phoebe" as mere whimsical indulgences in *As You Like It*; or "Chillingworth" and "Dimmesdale" and "Coverdale" in Hawthorne's novels. If they serve no other function, the names in *Rabbit, Run* warn the reader not to read the novel as a piece of simple realism; and they suggest from the beginning that the book is a type of fable, with satiric overtones.

Like its baffling epigraph, *Rabbit, Run* is ambiguous, absurd, and moving. But, perhaps first of all the novel is satiric and ironic. Bent on exposing Rabbit Angstrom's failure to return to innocence and nature, the satire and irony spring from those "built-in" reflexes to the pastoral attitude—the reflexes which lead to mock-pastoral and anti-pastoral satire. Essentially the same satiric responses which make us smile at, love, and pity the "holy innocents" Don Quixote and Gulliver also make us smile at, love, and pity Sinclair Lewis' George Babbitt and John Updike's Rabbit Angstrom. They are all on quests for something which the reader knows cannot be found or attained. In addition to pity, we also feel a certain amount of contempt for Rabbit Angstrom. Questers, eremites, and saints should be celibate, like St. Paul, Don Quixote, and Thoreau. For example, Gulliver's sojourn in the pastorally ideal land of the Houyhnhnms separates him from humanity, and leads him to live in the stables with the horses at the end of *Gulliver's Travels*. Rabbit's flight to nature similarly separates him from humanity, and causes him to run off into the woods at the end of *Rabbit, Run*. But if our pity and sympathy is primarily for Gulliver and Rabbit, it is perhaps misplaced; in pursuit of their solipsistic pastoral ideals, they both abandon savable wives and children.

In our time, the paucity of genuine tragedy and heroism in both life and fiction has led us carelessly to call the merely pathetic "tragic"; and our readiness to identify our sorrows with our fictional heroes' sorrows may cause us to become so involved in their *pathos* that we forget to smile at their *folly*. This is a real danger in reading *Rabbit, Run*, despite the rather leading facts that an *angstrom* is one ten-billionth of a meter, and the "hero" is, ultimately, a "Hairy Rabbit Angstrom." He who feels compassion mainly for Rabbit rather than his wife and children is in danger of being a sentimental tragedy-monger who has missed the cutting anti-pastoral satire of the novel.

The novel has a sad ending, a pathetic ending; deaths of infants, imminent abortions, abandoned and neglected children can never, by any sophisticated intellectual appeal to irony or paradox, be funny or comic. But satire, by its very nature, is not a "pure genre," as comic parody and classical tragedy, for example, are "pure." If anything, satire is profoundly earthy, pragmatic, and moral, and deals with the important middle ground between comedy and tragedy. Both Updike's *Rabbit, Run* and Swift's "A Modest Proposal" talk about the deaths of infants, and the moral injunctions and pragmatic didacticism of both would seem indisputably clear. Yet critics and reviewers often like to talk quite seriously about twenty-six-year-old Rabbit Angstrom as an existentialist-sensitive-young-man-on-a-spiritual-quest, as if his decision to "Ah: run. Run." were little more than fifteen-year-old Huck Finn's decision to "light out for the territory." Treating Rabbit's quest as if it were philosophically valid, and interpreting the novel's epigraph as a cryptic *excuse for* Rabbit's behavior rather than as an *explanation of* such behavior, readers and critics often say much about Rabbit's theology, and little about his relationship to his two-year-old son. By giving us glimpses of the child throughout the novel, and by showing us how seldom Rabbit thinks of him, Updike shows that Rabbit's main sin is that he "has left undone those things he ought to have done." Tacitly de-emphasizing Rabbit's role as an antihero, readers and critics tend to talk about Rabbit's sorrow and tragedy rather than his son Nelson's. Like the characters of *Couples*, who would be "like nymphs and satyrs in a grove, except for the group of distressed and neglected children," Rabbit would be a sensitive pastoral swain, justified in his heroic flight from his alcoholic "dumb" wife, except for his distressed and neglected child (his "Knell-son"?). I submit that the satire of the novel should be emphasized as fully as the pathos; and this satire is perhaps most clear in the treatment of the "return to nature" motif in the novel. That the satirical elements exist by no means makes the pathos and poignancy less immediate or less painful—if anything, these elements increase the novel's value as a portrayal of what Updike calls "the mixed stuff of human existence." [4]

Updike, himself an accomplished and slashing parodist

and comic satirist,[5] has written a telling essay on the function of laughter and satire in relation to pathos and seriousness: the essay is "Beerbohm and Others," collected in *Assorted Prose* (Knopf, 1965). In it he observes that the decline of parody and comedy as a distinctive genre, and the subsequent mingling of pathos and laughter may be a "symptom of recovery from nuclearphobia, cold war chilblains, hardening of the emotional arteries, and so forth."

Laughter is but one of many potential human responses; to isolate humor as a separate literary strain is as unnatural as to extract a genre of pathos or of nobility from the mixed stuff of human existence. Insofar as "serious" literature is indeed exclusively serious, then humor, as in the Victorian age, was a duty, in the Parliament of Man, to act as the loyal opposition. But when, as in this century, the absurd, the comic, the low, the dry, and the witty are reinstated in the imaginative masterworks, then humor as such runs the risk of becoming merely trivial, merely recreational, merely distracting. A skull constantly grins, and in the constant humorist there is a detachment and dandyism of the spirit whose temporary abeyance in this country need not be cause for unmitigated lamenting.[6]

Thus, the satirical elements of *Rabbit, Run* and *Couples* can be related to that "grinning skull," especially since infant deaths and abortions are involved in the ends of both novels. Indeed, Updike's work can be associated to some extent with the whole body of recent work currently referred to as "black humor." Unfortunately, the term is often used as if this were a twentieth-century phenomenon, a modern discovery that life is a mixture of horror and lyricism, pathos and laughter—as if the satiric and ironic treatment of pain, death, and damnation were not as old as Chaucer's "The Pardoner's Tale" and "The Sumonour's Tale," Shakespeare's *Hamlet*, Swift's "A Modest Proposal" and *Gulliver's Travels*, Voltaire's *Candide*, and Dickens' *Bleak House*. "Black humor" is merely a new name for an old technique, but the fact that recent fiction has prompted a renewed interest in the technique may, as Updike says, be a "symptom of recovery."

In the opening chapter of this essay, I suggested that a work is anti-pastoral when it challenges, refutes, and exposes the fallacies behind the dream of a return to nature. I also suggested that the concept of an elemental, simple life in a state of nature is a part of the American Dream and agrarian myth. Much of Rabbit Angstrom's failure can be attributed to his passionate pursuit of this ideal—an ideal which involves being in harmony with nature, rather than knowing one's relationship to nature. Those simple shepherds in the Theocritan *Idyls* were wonderfully adept at *being*, although their skill at *doing* and *knowing* was (to understate the case) limited. In terms of modern discussions about "essence" and "existence," they were wonderfully "existential." [7] No philosophical dialogues about the nature of God in Arcady; no soul-searching with priests between lyrical sexual encounters; no need to be concerned with the wages of sin in a place where sin does not exist.

First of all, Rabbit Angstrom is satirized through his very name, and through his inflated ideas of his past accomplishments. In assigning him the name "Rabbit," Updike associates him with a delicate, skittish, unintelligent and untrainable little animal noted for its prodigious breeding habits. In fright, which is often, it runs in circles. This process itself, i.e., equating a human with a certain animal, is an old satiric device as ancient as Aesop's *Fables*. The most common verbal associations with rabbits are "to be scared as a rabbit," and "to breed like rabbits"; secondary connotations are the soft, cute little anthropomorphic "Uncle Wigglys" and "Peter Rabbits" of children's fiction. Rabbit Angstrom's sensing he is in a "trap," his driving in a large circle, his fingering of his "lettuce," his following of his senses and animal intuitions, and so forth, are the linguistic tricks of fable, rather than, say, Howellsian Realism. The name and the rather farfetched symbolic details are part of an elaborate metaphor—rather in the way Aesop's *Fables* are metaphors, or Ben Jonson's *Volpone*, or Swift's "Houyhnhnms" in *Gulliver's Travels*, or D. H. Lawrence's "The Fox." In terms of the "return to nature" theme in *Rabbit, Run*, then, the metaphor suggests that

Harry, as a Rabbit, is already an animalistic part of nature; never quite having become fully human, he has little humanity to lose. The reader sees a far greater need for him to nurture a superego than for him to indulge his already overactive id. Rabbit's illusions of grandeur about his single real accomplishment in life (that is, once setting a high school basketball scoring record—since broken) also suggests satire.

To finally reduce Rabbit's personality and his quest to the absurd and irrelevant, Updike gives Rabbit a proper name suggesting measurements in ten-billionths of a meter. Not only is he reduced to the level of a minor animal, but he is also reduced into an infinitessimally small rabbit —a kind of animal cipher. And, to complete the satiric pattern of making the tiny and insignificant seem grand and heroic, Updike causes Rabbit to see his flight from responsibility as a quest for ultimate meaning—for what Rabbit himself describes, with inspired vagueness, as "this thing." [8]

"This thing" Rabbit longs for and runs toward is the lyrical simplicity of his adolescence—that is, his past glory as a high school basketball hero, and the exquisite titillation of exploratory sexuality. He has not realized that his youthful swainship is over—that Olinger (here Mount Judge) is a "state of mind." It is not enough to say that Rabbit is immature and an idealist; even Tothero tells him that. What is more important is that Rabbit still vaguely believes in the pastoral American Dream of eternal youth and transcendental harmony with nature. Escape. In terms of the American pastoral and anti-pastoral pattern, Rabbit is aligned with Thomas Morton's maypolers at Merry Mount —i.e., with sensuality and sexuality in Arcadia, rather than with Bradford's civilizing and disciplined Puritanism in Plymouth Plantation.

When Rabbit first runs at the beginning of the novel, he

wants to go south, down, down the map into orange groves and smoking rivers and barefoot women. It seems simple enough, drive all night through the dawn through the morning through the noon park on a beach take off your shoes and fall asleep by the Gulf of Mexico. Wake up with the stars above perfectly spaced in perfect health. [9]

This is a version of the pastoral dream, and it is little wonder that he dreams it. For example, as he flees from his pregnant alcoholic wife and his small son, he is encouraged, consoled, and primed by the relentless idyllic lyricism of popular American culture. His car radio soothes him with songs about "Secret Love," "Autumn Leaves," and "fields of corn" where "it makes no mind no how . . . wihithout [sic] a song." [10] Agrarians singing in the fields; nymphs and swains secretly loving in the woods. Rabbit's "scalp contracts ecstatically" in response to these twentieth-century versions of the Theocritan *Idyl*. We are reminded of George F. Babbitt's dream of the "Fairy Child" and of "really living," i.e., "plunging through the forest, making camp in the Rockies, a grim and wordless caveman!" — "like in a movie." Neither Rabbit nor Babbitt understands that idyls exist only in art (popular songs and movies, for example), rather than in real life.

As Rabbit rushes outdoors in flight from his apartment and his intolerable marriage, he sees a street sign as a "two-petaled flower," and a fire hydrant as "a golden bush: a grove." [11] Driving toward the "dawn cottonfields" on this heavily symbolic night of the vernal equinox, Rabbit mentally equates the land with a woman.

> His problem is to get west and free of Baltimore-Washington, which like a two-headed dog guards the costal route to the south. He doesn't want to go down along the water anyway, his image is of himself going right down the middle, right into the broad soft belly of the land, surprising the dawn cottonfields with his northern plates. [12]

He envies an adolescent couple in West Virginia, and he gets lost in a park which turns out to be a lovers' lane. His tendency to see himself as a "lover" who wants sexual intercourse to be "natural," without "devices," is part of his image of himself as an amorous swain. The irony is that his attitude toward sex is more a rabbit's attitude than a sensitive human being's. Furthermore, Rabbit's pastoral vision engenders "pathetic fallacies" in more than a literary sense; it is pathetic in that it eventually leads to moral anarchy, terror, and death. Again, this is part of the American tradition in the pastoral pattern, dating back to Thomas Morton's eventual armament of the Indians. Seeing "two-petaled" street signs and "golden bush" fire hydrants is like seeing an untamed wilderness as a paradise. It is a lie; and John Updike seems to be asserting that it is a dangerous lie.

Further related to Rabbit's doggedly idealized vision of nature is his refusal to see rural life and nature as it really is; by this I mean that he has contempt for real farmers and the unattractive earthiness of real rural life. Without comprehending it himself, he wants "snowy flocks" and "naked girls on the seashore," rather than dirty sheep and manure piles. At first he idealizes the rural farmer who fills his gas tank—he sees him as honest and law-abiding in a way that urban station attendants are not: "Laws aren't ghosts in this country, they walk around with the smell of earth on them." Then he discovers the farmer is drunk, and therefore corrupted; he doesn't fit Rabbit's pastoral ideal. Later, Rabbit, lost and circling back home, "blames everything on that farmer with glasses and two shirts." [13] Similarly, Rabbit at first idealizes an Amish couple in a horsedrawn buggy, and then mentally rejects them because their rural life is not ideal enough: First they are leading the "good life," "clear of all this phony business." Then they become "fanatics" who "worship manure." [14]

Perhaps the most telling facts about Rabbit's return to nature are the types of nature he returns to— 1) in his all-night drive toward the "broad soft belly of the land," he never really leaves his car; 2) in his walk into the woods with the prostitute Ruth, after their first night together, he climbs up man-made steps and comes out in a parking lot; 3) in his conversations with the Episcopal priest Eccles, he returns to the "groves" of a man-made golf course; and 4) in his occupation as a gardener, he works on a luxurious estate raising exotic rhododendrons. Thus, he never gets close to real farms and agrarians. Significantly, the park, the green, the garden are about as far as Rabbit gets on his return to nature—not much further than the classic English "village green" with its maypole in the middle.

Rabbit has never really grown any older than the high school basketball hero he was as a teenager. His sexual fantasies about his first girl friends, his premarital sex with his wife, and even his relationship with Ruth are all idyllic norms against which he judges his happiness. His first night with the prostitute Ruth is a high point for him. Significantly, Updike ends the incident with a pastoral image— clearly satiric since it is purely from the narrator's point of view rather than Rabbit's. "He is asleep when *like a faun in moonlight* Ruth, washed, creeps back to his side, holding a glass of water." [15] This image is important because Rabbit and Ruth have temporarily played the roles of nymph and satyr this night. But in order to do so, they have become moral anarchists: Rabbit has abandoned all familial and social responsibilities, and Ruth has sold her body to him.

The next day, nymph and satyr that they are, they make an excursion into Arcadian groves—the city park on the side of Mount Judge. However, since Rabbit and Ruth are corrupted, pseudo-Arcadians, their groves are also corrupted, haunted with thugs by night, and strewn with litter by day. The city park is shabby and joyless; "the ornamental pool in front of the bandshell is drained and scum-stained." [16] The effect is similar to T. S. Eliot's use of pastoral and anti-pastoral ironies in *The Waste Land*, where Elizabethan lyricism is contrasted to twentieth-century aridity. Having shown Ruth as "a faun in moonlight" and having shown Rabbit as the young swain, Updike then presents the trip into the park as a parody of the frolic in the pastoral grove. The description is satiric anti-pastoralism which establishes the discrepancy between the lyrical ideal and the tawdry reality. The couple take off their shoes and climb upward to the top of Mount Judge. At the top, in a parking lot, Rabbit looks over the city and is "bothered by God." He contemplates the inexorable power of death, and then, childlike, asks Ruth to put her arm around him. Then, in the satiric anticlimax, the ironic non sequitur,

Updike curtly sums up the prevailing anti-pastoral tone of the entire incident: "They take a bus down." [17]

The relationship between Eccles, the Episcopalian *ecclesiast*, and Rabbit is similarly a part of the pastoral and anti-pastoral pattern of the book. Eccles is the heir of two traditions: 1) his grandfather's, a Unitarian transcendentalist who believed that "God is in the woods," and 2) his father's, a reactionary orthodox Anglo-Catholic. To the extent that he follows the forms of his church, Eccles is orthodox; to the extent that he liberally tries to see men as basically good and redeemable through individual transcendence, he is an Emersonian transcendentalist. As Jimmy, the "Big Mouseketeer" on television, translates "know thyself" into "be yourself," Eccles translates the King James pronouncement "love faileth not" into the New World Translation version "love never ends." Eccles is a romantic transcendentalist who finally admits, after his failure with Rabbit, that he has no faith.

And, of course, in terms of the American tradition, Eccles is the perfect sympathetic audience for Rabbit's pastoral vision. Ironically warning Rabbit that "all vagrants think they're on a quest, at least at first," Eccles doesn't seem to realize that he himself treats Rabbit as if Rabbit's quest were a valid one.[18] Eccles plays golf with him, gets him a job, discusses philosophy with him, but says little about sin, morality, and responsibility. Kindred souls, the two men clearly show the close relationship between Emersonian transcendentalism and the classic pastoral ideal. Both dream of Eden.

Rabbit's quest is satirized through an accident of gesture: when trying to explain to Eccles that he is seeking the mystery within and behind nature, Angstrom inarticulately gestures out of the car window toward what he means to be the unspoiled landscape. Eccles has just delivered Rabbit a mini-sermon about "outer darkness" and "inner darkness."

Eccles' volunteering all this melts Rabbit's caution. He wants to bring something of himself into the space between them. The excitement of friendship, a competitive excitement that makes him lift his hands and jiggle them as if thoughts were basketballs, presses him to say, "Well I don't know all this about theology, but I'll tell you. I *do* feel, I guess, that somewhere behind all this"—he gestures outward at the scenery; they are passing the housing development this side of the golf course, half-wood half brick one-and-a-half-stories in little flat bulldozed yards with tricycles and spindly three-year-old trees, the ungrandest landscape in the world—"there's something that wants me to find it." [19]

Ironically, "all this" is meant to be idyllic nature. Again, the effect is satiric anticlimax. It is later, in the groves of the golf course, that Rabbit explains to Eccles that he is searching for "this thing."

The equation of transcendentalism with pastoralism, and Puritanism with anti-pastoralism also exists in the novel. Eccles, the Episcopalian, is pitted against Kruppenbach, the Lutheran minister. Kruppenbach, for all the narrowness of his vision, comes closer to being right about Rabbit than anybody else in the novel. Darkly Puritanical, he believes in sin and repentance; he takes the occasion of discussing Rabbit's "case" to attack Eccles for Eccles' own laxity and sentimentality. Howard M. Harper has rightly suggested that Kruppenbach's solution is "saner" than Eccles':

Despite Kruppenbach's lack of interest in Rabbit's "case," his view, Updike seems to suggest, is saner than Eccles' ineffectual meddling. Kruppenbach talks of the force of belief, and it is the quality of *force* which Rabbit admires most in people. Kruppenbach and Eccles, then, objectify two religious alternatives: one which Rabbit admires but cannot reach, the other which envelops him in its do-goodism but which he cannot respect.[20]

In terms of the American pastoral and anti-pastoral tradition, Kruppenbach would cut down the maypole and force reformation, whereas Eccles secretly tends to want to join the "frisking."

The rabbit takes a job gardening in old Mrs. Harry Smith's fancy rhododendron patch, the lavish garden on her wealthy estate. The garden is a version of Eden even to a direct comparison: an old woman had once told Mrs.

Smith that "heaven must be like this." Mrs. Smith is a realist who prefers alfalfa to expensively unique flowers. Her dead husband, not she, had been the idealizing pastoralist. Rabbit becomes a type of surrogate for her lost husband, also named Harry. Rabbit feels the old woman is in love with him—*wants* her to be in love with him. And here we have curiously grotesque scenes in which the ex-basketball-hero and the ancient dowager stroll through the Edenic lanes arm-in-arm, at peace. Perhaps the strangest Adam and Eve in literature. The gardens in May are cloyingly lush, and Rabbit uses the perfume to prime fantasies of nymphs. Rabbit dreams of a type of girl "he had often wanted and never had, a little Catholic from a shabby house, dressed in cheap bargain clothes." [21] Rabbit really believes such lusciously innocent girls exist; unfortunately, he does not realize that they exist chiefly on Grecian urns and on the slopes of Arcadia. Finally, Rabbit is disillusioned with the ancient Mrs. Smith for the same reason he was disillusioned with the farmer station attendant and the Amish couple: they and Mrs. Smith represent the *real* agrarian world. Mrs. Smith, a farmer's daughter, prefers alfalfa and buckwheat crops to flower beds. She is too earthy for Rabbit's taste. The idyllic "little Catholic" is the dream; the wrinkled old woman is the reality.

Finally, with the depressing end to the novel, Updike seems to be saying that Rabbit's pastoral vision has devastating results. The Theocritan *Idyl* idealizes the past in a dangerous way; that is, the attitude becomes dangerous when it is confused with reality, as it is in Rabbit Angstrom's mind. Rabbit's dream is the dream of eternal youth and immortality, the pastoral dream of "Heaven on Earth." His innocence is "radical" in the way Ihab Hassan defines it:

The anarchy in the American soul is nourished on an old dream: not freedom, not power, not even love, but the dream of immortality. America has never really acknowledged Time. Its vision of Eden or Utopia is essentially a timeless vision. Its innocence is neither geographical nor moral: it is mainly temporal, hence metaphysical. This is radical innocence. [22]

Updike sympathetically celebrates that innocence, if any-where, in his Olinger stories, not in *Rabbit, Run*. Simply that it is an American tradition is not enough to ameliorate its serious moral consequences. As Updike and other realists keep asserting, failure to acknowledge time results in failure to grow.

Thus, Rabbit is not a sympathetic hero on a quest, despite the allowances critics may make for him. Certainly, he makes an oversupply of allowances for himself. Perhaps the most charitable reading of the moral tensions in *Rabbit, Run* is William Van O'Connor's conclusion that Rabbit is no worse than the other characters in the novel.

Presumably, Updike is not saying that Rabbit Angstrom is following the only honest course in rejecting the sententious platitudes offered him. The novel catches many little ironies — Rabbit's notion that he is praising his coach when he is praising himself, or the minister's wanting a glass of water while consol-ing Mrs. Springer, and many others. Human motives and actions show a welter of inconsistencies. But there are certain con-sistencies: Eccles is something of an ass, but he does help cer-tain people; Ruth, the prostitute, is quite capable of loyalty and devotion, and, in her own way, maintains her self-respect. Jan-ice is terribly weak, but she wants to make a go of her marriage. Tothero is a dirty old man, physically and mentally, but he'd prefer not to be, and his advice is on the side of the angels. The novel seems not to be saying that man's moral gestures are all fraudulent. It could even be saying, with Auden, *Love your crooked neighbor with your crooked heart*.[23]

In terms of the body of Updike's work, I believe this con-clusion is perhaps too generous toward the characters, and especially toward Rabbit. Rabbit has an intelligence and sensibility which make him singularly responsible for his actions. It is not "external circumstances" which separate Rabbit from "the motions of [God's] Grace"; rather, it is "the hardness of the heart," which, I take it, is a result of willful moral acts, and not deterministic accidents. Rab-bit is worse than the other characters.

The satirical anti-pastoral elements of the novel are re-lated to the moral theme. Essentially, Rabbit is like the hero of Nathanael West's *Miss Lonelyhearts*, as described in a critical essay by Roger D. Abrahams: *"Miss Lonelyhearts* is a novel of psychological development, one we might call the 'existential,' the 'chaotic experience,' or the antiromance novel." Abrahams continues,

Here isolation is a permanent condition; the progress of the psyche, if there is any, is toward more intensive isolation, perhaps death. The tone of such works is ironic. Moments occur which might have become revelatory but which fail to transform the protagonist or resolve his problems. Consequently, the protagonist is never able to achieve the object of his search, the ability to act. He is immobilized. The search becomes a wait. This kind of progression characterizes *Miss Lonelyhearts.* The fixed moral and psychological dilemma of man is morbidly attractive; his search for answers is necessary but futile.[24]

The comments are pointedly applicable to Rabbit Angstrom's character. Rabbit's sin—the one which results in "the hardness of the heart"—is his solipsistic refusal to see himself as a sinner. Ready to condemn his fellows, he seems to be constantly thankful that he is not as they are. In fact, his self-righteous search for youth and innocence makes him more of a sinner than any of the others; it is an exorbitant and damning form of pride. In his search for Eden, he appears to himself as an innocent victim of a corrupt society.

As in so many satires, a moral point of view is developed through the presentation of an innocent in the midst of the corrupt, corruption appearing that much more profound because it is presented by the naive observer. Further, the innocent is shown to be fully as deluded and vain as the corrupt; just as we discover that such satiric protagonists as Gulliver and Candide are the dupes of their own insular systems of thought, so Miss Lonelyhearts [and Rabbit Angstrom] is revealed to be deluded by his mystical sentimentalism.[25]

The ending of *Rabbit, Run* involves the melodramatic death of Rabbit's infant daughter, who slips out of his drunken wife's hands and drowns in the bathtub. It is an indefensible and exaggerated stroke of melodrama only if we forget the other exaggerations in the novel—the name puns and the parodic pastoral imagery, for example. Stylistically, the book is a mixture of moral fable and realism. The death is overdrawn in the way fables, allegories, and morality plays are overdrawn—as a symbol of the consequences of Rabbit's romantic view of the world. Driven by guilt to protest too much at the funeral, Rabbit is compelled to blurt out his innocence, and then run into the woods. He later seeks out Ruth, discovers that she is pregnant by him and considering an abortion, and then "he runs. Ah, runs: Runs."

In an excellent short article entitled "*Rabbit Run:* John Updike's Criticism of the 'Return to Nature,' " Gerry Brenner arrives at the crux of the novel. Substantially, the only difference between my conclusions about the nature theme, and Gerry Brenner's conclusions is that I extend the subject to an historical tradition of pastoral and anti-pastoral patterns. Otherwise, we are in complete accordance. A portion of the Brenner essay merits lengthy quotation:

Updike's focus upon the consequences of Rabbit's unconsidered blithe actions criticizes with calm insistence the omnipresent desire to "return to nature" by showing the logical extension of that desire. More, he shows that instead of just a vague romantic ideal, it has become an integrated part of reality. Like all the values whose worth has depreciated in the twentieth century, the value of returning to nature, for example, has been immersed in the world of daily action, a colloquialization of the ideal. And made accessible, it is adulterated and abused until it is converted into a distorted way of life. The ideas of the past, which have value *precisely because* they spur effort for attainable goals, have become misinterpreted (like the "be yourself" interpretation of "Know Thyself"), debased (like the anarchy of authority), and pursued unconsciously without understanding. Now that the ideal has been lost, Updike suggests that a practiced return to nature, carried to its logical conclusion, ends in destruction. . . . The return to nature, like all impoverished ideas, is wrenched out of its original context and thrust into an alien situation. In the original context, the return was only to geographical nature. In the present-day context, the return has been to a psychological nature of physical impulse, lacking external, prescriptive refinements. The shadow of neanderthal man clearly hangs over modern man who, like Rabbit, possesses more id (in his impulse for nature) than ego, and possesses only wisps of a super-ego.

Updike's philosophical conservatism conceives of the romantic dream of returning to nature, in its worst sense, as the ultimate extension of the loss of traditional values, ideals, laws. Set into a society that persists in adhering to some prescriptive mores, Rabbit, as a "noble" urban savage, images modern man's tradition-less character and portends his concomitant problems. And the effectiveness of the novel resides in Updike's projection of this statement through the use of the tacky social setting and a line-up of only moderately sympathetic characters.[26]

Those "external, prescriptive refinements" which Rabbit lacks are partly the sophistication and erudition required for seeing a return to nature in its historical context; that is, to see it in the tradition of Theocritus and Thoreau. The oldest myth in the Hebraic-Christian tradition is the myth of the loss of Eden; placed as it is, hard on the heels of the story of the creation of the race itself, this *should* be the first lesson Western man learns. It seems to be the last. The entire American tradition, from *The New English Canaan* to *Rabbit, Run*, contains characters who, like Theocritus two thousand years earlier, refuse to accept the loss of Eden as an inexorable fact, and consequently create Edens and Idyls in art and in their minds. Where is Rabbit Angstrom running to? To Olinger. And Updike has explained to us that Olinger is a "state of mind"—"like a town in a fable." Rabbit expects to find it physically, like finding a geographical location here on earth. Despite his ambiguity and subtlety, one point which John Updike makes painfully clear in the body of his fiction is that Rabbit Angstroms of the world will ultimately fail, no matter how long and how far they "Ah: run. Run."

5

The Centaur
Epic Paean and Pastoral Lament

For John Milton to have transformed the Cambridge scholar Edward King into the simple shepherd Lycidas in order to ennoble and aggrandise him is a curious inversion of the Hebraic-Christian tradition by which great kings of earth and gods of heaven are shepherd boys (King David of the Old Testament) and humble peasants born in mangers (Jesus of the New Testament). In the Hellenistic tradition, kings and gods are also often disguised as shepherds (for example, Apollo and Paris); and the gods themselves are nagging housewives (Hera), promiscuous husbands (Zeus), blacksmiths (Haephestus), and so forth. The process of linking pastoral simplicity and epic grandeur, along with its pervasive inversion, seems to be a preoccupation within the myths of the Western world. The paradox is central to the entire story of Jesus and his teachings. And far from diminishment, the process has, if anything, been reinforced within the American democratic tradition. In terms of the classic pastoral-epic metaphor, for Abraham Lincoln to have been born in a log cabin on the frontier is as essential to the wholeness of "the myth of Lincoln" as Jesus' birth in a manger is to the wholeness of "the myth of Jesus." Indeed, even in our more minor American myths, we still like our presidents to be simple Quakers from Yorba Linda, ex-country-school-teachers from Texas, or the elegant Bostonian sons of once-poor Irish immigrants. The mind delights in linking the humble with the grand. Theocritus of Alexandria worked in two genres only—pastoral and epic;[1] Virgil is known for his *Eclogues* and his *Aeneid,* as Milton is best known for *Lycidas* and *Paradise Lost.*

John Updike's finest work—the novel which would have established him as a "major" writer, had he written nothing else—rests directly in the mainstream of this pastoral-epic pattern; furthermore, *The Centaur* powerfully illuminates the pattern itself. Rather than merely using the metaphor, Updike contributes to it in the way that James Joyce and John Milton, for example, contributed to it—Milton in adding Christianity, and Joyce in adding post-Darwinian and post-Freudian philosophy. Why are the apparently contradictory and dichotomous pastoral and epic metaphors so important to Western culture, and to the race itself? John Updike's epigraph to *The Centaur* provides part of the answer; his novel provides the rest. The epigraph is a quotation from the theologian Karl Barth:

Heaven is the creation inconceivable to man, earth the creation conceivable to him. He himself is the creature on the boundary between heaven and earth.

Ipso facto, two creations exist, call them what one will—heavenly and earthly, spiritual and material, ideal and real, unconscious and conscious, imaginative and empirical, divine and temporal, epic and pastoral—it does not matter. Man, unable to conceive one of the creations, employs earth, that creation which he can conceive, to explain the other. Ingenious and ironic animal that he is, he creates exaggerated metaphors befitting his exaggerated, rather absurd position of being "on the boundary between heaven and earth." Unable to conceive a ruler of that other creation, he makes god into an exaggerated version of his earthly father, who, as he knows from experience, is capable of both extreme mercy and extreme wrath. Conscious that the role of the shepherd is the lowliest earthly social position, he causes his god to be born in a stable and to become "the good shepherd" as well as "the Son of God." And in an inspired burst of irony, he dresses his popes and bishops (symbolic intermediaries who are kinds of walking metaphors assigned to zigzag across the boundary) in splendid robes, and thrusts a shepherd's crook into their hands—a *golden* shepherd's crook. Or he makes the brightest god of Olympus, Phoebus Apollo, serve Admetus for a year as a slave; his heroes cleanse stables and cook their own suppers. He places a man's torso on a horse's body, and makes him the teacher of the gods. His saviors are ironically thieves and drifters, stealing fire from the gods and telling paradoxical parables on mountainsides. But in their willingness to suffer on rocks and crosses, in their ability to fully penetrate both the conceivable and inconceivable creations, they become the best comfort that man has. The reciprocal sliding scale between epic and pastoral, I take it, is one way of metaphorically reconciling the imponderable paradoxes involved in the human condition of being "a little lower than the angels" and a little higher than the beasts —like a Centaur. Chiron, The Centaur, half man and half horse, can be seen as the perfect symbol for the paradoxical union of epic and pastoral patterns in Updike's novel. Epically, Chiron makes the grand sacrificial gesture which propitiates the crime of the hero Prometheus, and sets him free; pastorally, Chiron teaches the children of the gods in Arcadian groves.

The art of *The Centaur* depends on structure as fully as it depends on theme and metaphor. Indeed, the basic metaphor which compares Olinger citizens to Olympian citizens would merely be a kind of tour de force, a brilliant exercise in analogy and allegory comparable to, say, *Pilgrim's Progress*, were it not for the structure of the novel. Without Updike's arrangement of chapters and his knowledgeable employment of juxtaposed modes and traditions, the surrealism of *The Centaur* would be merely arrestingly clever —like a fur-lined teacup, or a Salvador Dali painting; in Wordsworthian terms, it would be "fanciful" rather than creatively "imaginative." The structure depends on the fact that four interspersed short chapters of the book establish the total work as a "pastoral elegy," as certainly and as imaginatively as *Lycidas* is a pastoral elegy. Furthermore, Updike becomes a classicist in writing this novel—in the sense that Milton is a classicist, as opposed to the sense in which eighteenth-century English Augustans were classical. The difference, I take it, is that Milton strove for and achieved the *spirit* of the pastoral, epic, and tragic modes, rather than copying the form and letter of the originals: it is Alexander Pope's and Edward Young's distinction — the difference between imitating Homer and Theocritus rather than the *Iliad* and the *Idyls*.

In *The Centaur*, chapters 3, 5, 8, and 9 are all variations of basic conventions of the traditional pastoral elegy. They stand out in the novel because of their brevity and their abrupt tonal shifts. The rest of the novel (the longer chapters 1, 2, 4, 6, and 7) tells the story of the three days Peter-Prometheus and his father George Caldwell-Centaur spend in town, snowed in and unable to return to the mother Ceres and the home farm. The four pastoral chapters declare themselves as legitimate elements of the traditional pastoral elegy through 1) correspondence of conventional subject matter, and 2) correspondence of conventional language and imagery. As to subject matter, the pattern works as follows:

1) Chapter 3, only five pages long, shows the pastoral hero Chiron involved in his daily tasks of teaching the children of the gods in Arcadian groves. Idyllic in the strictest sense, the passage includes a conventional catalogue of flowers and herbs and celebrates the tranquility and beauty of the hero as he was in life. Roughly, it corresponds to lines 25–36 of *Lycidas*.

2) Chapter 5, four pages long, is a newspaper obituary, giving a coldly factual account of Caldwell's life. It suggests the conventional expression of communal grief. It is the elegiac announcement of death, roughly comparable to the flat shock value of the fact, "For Lycidas is dead, dead ere his prime," lines 10 and following of *Lycidas*.

3) Chapter 8 (the first four pages), is the expression of Peter's personal grief for the loss of the pastoral hero. Here

Peter-Prometheus sings his lament to his Negro mistress. He questions the meaning of his father's death in a version of the elegiac interrogation of the universe, roughly analagous to lines 50–85 of *Lycidas*.

4)   Chapter 9, four pages long, is a consolation and reconciliation, an account of the Centaur's acceptance of death, and his son's reconciliation to it. The short epilogue is an account of the Centaur's apotheosis as a star. Roughly, it corresponds to lines 165–93 of *Lycidas*.

The structural continuity of these seemingly fragmented chapters provides the touchstone necessary for reading the entire novel, for seeing it as a unified whole. Boldly shifting from Olinger to Olympus would be comic, like mock-epic, if it were not for Updike's employment of the conventions of the pastoral elegy.

The language of these touchstone chapters provides the lyricism and formality required to keep the novel from being ironic, satiric, and comic. Seen as a highly personal expression of both Updike's and Peter's sense of loss (Updike has left Shillington to become a writer for the *New Yorker*, and Peter is painting abstractions in a New York loft), *The Centaur* appeals to the impersonality of stock pastoral conventions as a vehicle for transforming life into art— the personal into the universal. The very stockness of the language in these chapters—from the idyllic song and catalogue in chapter 3, to the journalistic jargon in chapter 5, to the mixture of love lyric and lament in chapter 8, to the elevated statement of apotheosis in the epilogue,—provides a stable point of reference for the almost schizophrenic imagery shifts and linguistic jerks in the rest of the novel. When we come to chapter 3, we recognize the purely stock language and subject matter of the Theocritan pastoral, and we can rest; when we arrive at chapter 5, we almost gratefully recognize the stock jargon of obituaries, and so forth. Grief and loss must be pinned down and stabilized if perspective and sanity are to be retained. Formal language —even to the point of *stock* language—is needed to accompany that "formal feeling" which Emily Dickinson says comes "after great pain." This, I take it, is the purpose of the language of rites and ceremonies—the rationale behind the language of eulogies, obituaries, and pastoral elegies.

Explicitly Arcadian in the strictest classical sense, chapter 3 subtly merges pastoral description with a paean to the gods, "slim pale reeds of a single pipe harmoniously hymning the god of existence pure." [2] Thus, even in this passage Updike merges the pastoral with the heroic, the catalogue of flowers and herbs with the epic paean. The conventional language of the passage is, in kind, straight out of Theocritus' *Idyls*. Compare the stock language of Updike's idyl and Theocritus' idyl. From Updike:

Chiron hurried, a little late, down the corridors of tamarisk, yew, bay, and kermes oak. Beneath the cedars and silver firs, whose hushed heads were shadows permeated with Olympian blue, a vigorous underwood of arbutus, wild pear, cornel, box, and andrachne filled with scents of flower and sap and new twig in the middle air of the forest. Branches of bloom here and there dashed color across the shifting caverns of forest space that enclosed the haste of his canter. He slowed. The ragged and muted attendants of air escorting his high head slowed also. These intervals of free space—touched by the arching search of fresh shoots and threaded by the quick dripdrop of birdsong released as if from a laden ceiling rich in elements (some songs were water, some copper, some silver, some burnished rods of wood, some cold and corrugated fire) —were reminiscent for him of caverns and soothed and suited his nature. His student's eyes—for what is a teacher but a student grown old?—retrieved, from their seclusion in the undergrowth, basil, hellebore, feverwort, spurge, polypody, bryony, wolf's-bane, and squill. Ixine, cinquefoil, sweet marjoram and gilliflower he lifted, by the shape of their petals, leaves, stems, and thorns, from their anonymity in indiscriminate green. Recognized, the plants seemed to lift crisply in salute, hailing the passage of a hero.[3]

From Theocritus:

Then they went forth upon the shore, and each couple busily got ready supper in the late evening, and many as they were one bed they strewed lowly on the ground, for they found a meadow lying, rich in couches of strown grass and leaves. Thence they cut them pointed flag-leaves, and deep marsh-galingale. And Hylas of the yellow hair, with a vessel of bronze in his hand, went to draw water against supper time, for Heracles himself, and the steadfast Telamon, for these comrades twain supped ever at one table. Soon was he ware of a spring, in a hollow land, and the rushes grew thickly round it, and dark swallowwort, and green maiden-hair, and blooming parsley, and deergrass spreading through the marshy land. In the midst of the water the nymphs were arraying their dances, the sleepless nymphs, dread goddesses of the country people, Eunice, and Malis, and Nycheia, with her April eyes.[4]

In chapter 3, the inclusion of the heroic hymn in the Homeric manner is a convention of one version of the Theocritan *Idyl*. For example, "Idyl 22" is a paean:

We hymn the children twain of Leda, and of aegis-bearing Zeus,—Castor, and Pollux, the boxer dread, when he hath harnessed his knuckles in thongs of oxhide. Twice hymn we, and thrice the stalwart sons of the daughter of Thestias, the two brethren of Lacedaemon.[5]

The echo in Updike is,

> Lord of the sky
> Wielder of weather,
> Brightness of brightness,
> Zeus, hear our song!
>
> Fill us with glory,
> Crest of the thunderhead,
> Shape us with gradualness,
> Source of the rain! [6]

Thus, Updike includes the highly conventional language of the Homeric chant. The result of this purely pastoral chapter is to establish a basis for the reading of the whole novel. The reader is calmed and soothed and reconciled by the familiar conventional language—he begins to think that there is some order to what is taking place in the novel— some coherence and meaning to it all. To this extent, the language of the four touchstone chapters is highly important. The chapters become the formal structural clues for reading the whole book. Idyl, hymn, obituary, love lyric, lament, epitaph—these recognizable forms within the pastoral elegy form give the novel its coherence, its dignity, its eloquence as a universal statement.

The first pages of chapter 8 are also pastoral. Here we find the combination of love lyric, pastoral reminiscence, lament, and interrogation of the universe. Here Peter speaks to his Negro mistress, and combines his love song for her with his memory of his father and Olinger. The reminiscent description of the Alton Museum employs language straight out of Theocritus:

> Quickly crossing the harsh width of a three-lane highway, we would enter on a narrow path the museum grounds, and an even older world, Arcadian, would envelop us. Ducks and frogs mixed flat throaty exultations in the scummy marsh half-hidden by the planted lines of cherry, linden, locust, and crab-apple trees.[7]

Explicitly "Arcadian" like the world of chapter 3, the museum and its grounds are associated with the "only treasury of culture accessible to us"—i.e., it is associated with *art*. In addition, the museum exists in ideal nature, in Arcady, as opposed to the harsh reality of real nature.

> In the basement, indeed, free classes in "nature appreciation" were held in the summer months. At my mother's suggestion I once enrolled. The first lesson was to watch a snake in a glass cage swallow a chattering field mouse whole. I did not go for the second lesson.[8]

The passage is important because Peter-Prometheus is now an artist in New York. The struggles of his parents, the sacrifices of his Centaur-Father, have been made so that Peter can be freed to be an artist. It is here that Peter questions the validity of such sacrifice. He sees the role of artist as a deterioration from that of priest and teacher: "Priest, teacher, artist: the classic degeneration." And he asks, "Was it for this that my father gave up his life?"[9] It is the type of question found in "Lycidas": "Where were ye nymphs . . . ?" and "What boots it with uncessant care/ To tend the homely slighted shepherd's trade . . . ?"

But his father The Centaur has given Peter-Prometheus

another gift—the ability to love. We see this in Peter's version of the love lyric to his mistress, which is interwoven with the interrogation of the meaning of his father's sacrifice:

Listen: I love you, love your prim bruised mouth whose corners compress morally when you are awake and scolding me, love your burnt skin ceaselessly forgiving mine, love the centuries of being humbled held in the lilac patina of your palms. I love the tulip-stem stance of your throat. When you stand before the stove you make, all unconscious, undulant motions with the upper half of your body like a drinking hen. When you walk naked toward the bed your feet toe in as if your ankles were manacled to those of someone behind you. When we make love sometimes you sigh my name and I feel radically confirmed.[10]

Like the language of the obituary of chapter 5, the language of this chapter is curiously stock; we can recognize the forms and idiosyncrasies rather in the way we recognize the cliches like, "The couple was blessed with two offspring, of which George was the second." [11] Though seemingly opposites, the language of newspaper obituary and the language of pastoral love lyric are, in kind, parts of the same pattern: in form and function, they relate to the pattern of elegiac pastoral conventions, as outlined above. In the way that the obituary serves as the required expression of communal and social grief, Peter's song to his love is a part of his expression of intense personal grief. Even in the prototypic Theocritan *Idyl*, the shepherd sings his lament to a close friend or lover.[12]

The final chapter of *The Centaur* provides the required consolation, and the one-sentence epilogue provides the conventional apotheosis. The acceptance of death is associated with the return to the rural home, to Ceres and the earth. It is winter, and the landscape contrasts to the warm pastoral scene of chapter 3. On the realistic level, we learn that George Caldwell does not have cancer as he had feared (at least, the x-rays show nothing); on the metaphoric level, we see Chiron's necessary death and his subsequent rebirth as a constellation. The pointed consolation is that "all joy belongs to the Lord," and that "only goodness lives." [13]

The final chapter is no longer a celebration of the beauty of the earth, with scenes from idealized pastoral nature. It is winter, the time of death. In this last chapter the imagery is based on the coupling of Uranus (sky) and Gaia (earth), heaven and earth. The union echoes Karl Barth's two "creations," the inconceivable and the conceivable. The coldness and bleakness of winter, the "brutish land-scape," are not so important now, because the Centaur is approaching death, and his apotheosis into the heavens. And in accepting his fate, he becomes the hero, the savior, the sacrificial figure who mediates between heaven and earth. Having provided the conventional consolation, Updike resorts to a Greek sentence to describe the death of Chiron. Translated, the sentence reads,

And having received an incurable wound, he went off to the cave. And he willingly went there to die; and although he was immortal and thus not able to die, when Prometheus exchanged fates with him, in order that Chiron might die in his stead, then the Centaur died.[14]

The inclusion of the Greek sentence between Chiron's final word, "*Now*," and the terminal statement, "Chiron accepted death," is a way of finally thrusting the novel back into the classical, primitive archetypes of the race. The story is not merely a myth retold, or a tribute to a good and noble man of our time; rather, it is an *old* story, originally told in Greek. It is the story of all sacrificial heroes who endure suffering and death for other men. It is the story, for example, of all fathers who have worked hard and devoted themselves to duty in order that their sons might have better lives than they have had.

Like Lycidas, who becomes a "genius of the shore," Chiron becomes the constellation Sagittarius. Apotheosis completes the novel as a pastoral elegy.

Thus, *The Centaur* achieves its aesthetic unity and thematic wholeness through the adaptation of elements of the traditional pastoral elegy. It is a brilliant and a bold adaptation; and, in its own way, the novel ranks with John Milton's adaptations of pastoral and epic modes. Updike follows the Horatian injunction that the artist improve on

his models. And I take it that the Horatian idea of im-
provement is partly a matter of historical immediacy—that
is, making a tradition valid and significant *for one's own
time*, a transmutation rather than a translation. John Milton
did this in writing a "Christian pastoral elegy"; John Updike does this in writing what might be called an "existentialist pastoral elegy." Both *Lycidas* and *The Centaur* are
eloquent tributes to the validity of the prototypic form.
This process of adapting the conventions of the pastoral
elegy to a contemporary theme is, itself, an American tradition aligned to Walt Whitman's "When Lilacs Last in the
Dooryard Bloom'd" and to James Agee's A *Death in the
Family*. For example, Updike's substitution of a newspaper
obituary for the traditional expression of communal mourn-
ing is not greatly different from Whitman's substituting a
funeral train for the traditional flower-decked bier. The
substitutions are alike in spirit and in kind.

Although he employs a version of the pastoral elegy for
the unifying structure of *The Centaur*, Updike deals with
the pastoral and anti-pastoral theme in still another way in
the novel. He continues the old pattern of the primary
tensions between rural and urban values—the tensions first
presented in the earlier *Olinger Stories* and in *Rabbit, Run*.
First, the Caldwell Farm is the same one we earlier en-
countered in "Pigeon Feathers." And it is the one we later
encounter in *Of the Farm*. In very real ways, the mother
and father in the story "Pigeon Feathers" are the mother
and father in *The Centaur*; and the young son is the
same. Updike's preoccupation with reconciling opposites
(heaven and earth, masculine and feminine, urban and
rural, for example) is further developed in *The Centaur* by
the facts that the intellectual, heroic Chiron is married to
Ceres, the goddess of the harvest and the earth. Ceres (or
Demeter) is mentioned more than any other deity in the
Theocritan *Idyls*. Half man and half horse, the Centaur is,
by his very nature, a conciliatory and unifying creature—
embodying the best of two worlds. Primarily a teacher,
scholar, and intellectual, he travels between the worlds of
matter and the worlds of mind and spirit. Symbolically,

he daily commutes from the farm to his teaching job in town. His marriage to Ceres is as essential to his horse's body as the academic world is to his man's torso. And he loves his wife, the earth, even as he shudders at her earthiness. In the realistic sections of the novel—i.e., those where the hero is clearly George Caldwell, rather than the Centaur Chiron—we find attitudes toward nature which seem to be contradictions. For example, Caldwell loves his wife, but hates the farm; he advises, "Don't take an animal out of nature," [15] but he also tells his wife, "I hate nature. It reminds me of death." [16] These attitudes *are* contradictory; but they are contradictions consistent with the basic contradictions which the Centaur embodies as half horse, half man. In a way, the Centaur, in both the Greek tradition and in Updike's adaptation, strangely represents the harmony of human and animal realms, rather than the conflict between them.

Chapter 2 of the novel realistically describes the life on the farm. Narrating the life to his mistress, Peter refuses to idealize or pastoralize that rural life. Still, it is one of the most beautiful portions of the novel; here we see affection and human interaction which cannot be found in the urban environment, at least in the rarefied ether of Olinger-Olympus. To the extent that Peter, as narrator, is looking back on the *entirety* of agrarian life (including both the farm and Olinger) from the standpoint of the alienated New York artist, the chapter is idyllic—like all the Olinger stories. It becomes a lament for something lost. But, at the same time, the farm is a reality *because* it is ugly as well as beautiful, as the Centaur himself is a beautiful grotesque. Whereas "the land represented purity" to the mother, it represented "rot and excrement" to Peter.[17] As in "Pigeon Feathers," the mother is associated with the feminine element, the earth, "Mother Ge." The son and the father revolt against the farm; mind and thought are masculine in Updike's fiction.

But the boy is perfectly willing to celebrate nature in the *ideal*—that is, pastorally. In the way that he had been repelled by the brutal "nature lesson" in the museum basement, he associates the real land and farming with "rot and excrement." In order to be made meaningful and unchaotic, nature for Peter must be transformed into art. On the morning before he and his father leave the farm for the three-day sojourn in the city, Peter contemplates a juvenile painting he had made of his old backyard, the yard belonging to the house in Olinger where the family had lived before moving to the country. The picture and Peter's feelings about it suggest the pastoral attitude: the artist and the pastoralist enjoy the ordered grace of a painted or created backyard more than the "rot and excrement" of "the land." Peter admires the painted landscape because it is a "potential fixing of a few passing seconds." [18] This comment on the purpose of art—the purposefully firm "potential fixing of a few passing seconds" —is as good an explanation of John Updike's Olinger stories and his fundamental lyricism as any reader or critic should desire; likewise, it is an adequate explanation of the aesthetics of Theocritan *Idyls*. At the end of *The Centaur*, the return of Peter and his father to the mother's farm, after staying in town three days, is connected with Peter's insight about art and nature: feverishly, the boy thinks,

The stone bare wall was a scumble of umber; my father's footsteps thumbs of white in white. I knew what this scene was—a patch of Pennsylvania in 1947—and yet I did not know, was in my softly fevered state mindlessly soaked in a rectangle of colored light. [*Sic*] I burned to paint it, just like that, in its puzzle of glory; it came upon me that I must go to Nature disarmed of perspective and stretch myself like a large transparent canvas upon her in the hope that, my submission being perfect, the imprint of a beautiful and useful truth would be taken.[19]

Prometheus is to be freed from his rock by Chiron's sacrifice; and he must be freed for some heroic task. In the novel, the equation of Peter with the artist suggests that the creation of Art is that heroic task. In several ways, the character of Peter-Prometheus is a "Portrait of the Artist as a Young Man," and he is like James Joyce's portrait of Stephen Dedalus—even to the extent of directly associating the artist in our time with the classical hero. Updike's *Olinger Stories* can be seen as forerunners to the epic-idyllic sweep of the surrealistic novel *The Centaur,* rather in the way Joyce's *Portrait of the Artist as a Young Man* can be seen as a forerunner to *Ulysses.* And both authors employ adaptations of classical mythology in their works. But in the way that Joyce's fiction as a whole is peculiarly Irish, Updike's fiction as a whole is peculiarly American—and that means that Updike must handle the "agrarian myth" in some way; he handles it by making it part of the far-reaching pastoral and anti-pastoral pattern in his fiction.

The matter of art is also related to Peter's hatred of "the land" in other passages in the book. This hatred of real farms and "the land" is perhaps more an "anti-agrarian" attitude than an "anti-pastoral" attitude. But, by the same token, Updike's refusal to idealize the farm itself (with its lack of plumbing, its chill and bleakness in winter, its inconveniences) is an element of anti-pastoralism in the book. Peter and his father flee "the land" each morning; on one symbolic level, this is flight from the femininity of matter (Ceres and the earth) to the masculinity of mind and spirit (Mount Olympus, the classroom, heaven). Peter's hatred of "the land" can be seen as a flight from his mother's domination—rather in the way Huck Finn's flight from "the land" is also flight from the domination of Miss Watson and the Widow Douglas. It is Peter's mother who arranges for those brutal "nature lessons" in the basements of museums and churches. And Peter escapes those stifling lessons on "cattle diseases and corn pests" by fleeing to his book of Vermeer reproductions.[20] Nature acted upon by art (the idealizing pastoral norm) is preferable to raw nature (the realistic and anti-pastoral norm).

The daily flight into Olinger-Olympus is associated with the safety of turning from the rutted dirt road onto the "firm macadam" of the highway. Highly symbolic, the action of either leaving the dirt road or turning onto it is always a clue to Updike's theme: for example, the first line of *Of the Farm* reads, "We turned off the Turnpike onto a macadam highway, then off the macadam onto a pink dirt road." In *The Centaur*, the pattern is especially complex. Although the son and father flee in the mornings, they look forward to returning in the evenings. Since Olinger is Mount Olympus, and therefore a version of "heaven," the daily trips back and forth from the farm suggest an integrated shuttling and familiarity with both heaven and earth, mind and matter, the "inconceivable creation" and the "conceivable creation." In addition, returning to the farm is like returning to the past—it is temporal as well as spatial. The mother, Ceres, symbolically wants to break the new red plastic clock her husband has bought for her.[21] She hates time, because the earth is timeless; she, like her farm and all it stands for, is a physical negation of the passage of time. Representing matter, she cannot be destroyed, but merely change in form, through the slow, clockless processes of erosion and decay, and subsequent recomposition and rebirth.

In his foreword to the *Olinger Stories*, Updike comments on his "Olinger Theme"; speaking of the collected stories, he says,

Not an autobiography, they have made one impossible. In the last of them, Olinger has become "like a town in a Fable"; and in my novel *The Centaur*, by turning Olinger explicitly into Olympus, I intended to say the final word, and farewell. Perhaps I exaggerate; it is an inherited fault.[22]

The "final word and farewell" to the memory of his youth and innocence requires the epic metaphors found in *The Centaur*. Employing a technique fundamental to a comic mode (i.e., mock-epic,), he tempers and molds the simple story of Peter and George Caldwell into the epic-idyllic story of Prometheus and Chiron. Aware that the elevation of rural rustics into heroic sophisticates is a tricky business, he follows Thoreau's technique of smiling first—of making the analogies and metamorphoses so striking and absurd that the reader's own imagination is engaged from the beginning, where the wounded Chiron walks down the hall and defecates in front of the high school trophy case.

Making the high school principal Zeus, and the girls' gym teacher Aphrodite is the kind of shocking artistic boldness that we find in Thoreau's *Walden,* where Thoreau makes the weeds of his bean patch into an epic army. In art, camels are often easier to swallow than gnats, and considerably more palatable. Then, after hitting the reader with his farfetched analogies, Updike structures the entire novel around the conventions of the traditional pastoral elegy—complete with the list of formal subjects, and versions of highly stock language. The result is *not* mock-epic and comic. Rather, because of the structural significance of the four interspersed "touchstone chapters," the novel retains the eloquence and dignity of an elegy. If there is any fundamental irony within the novel, it is not that Olinger becomes Olympus, and that George Caldwell is explicitly metamorphosed into the heroic Centaur; rather, it is that human beings so easily overlook genuine heroism when they see it. The difference between genuine heroism and pseudo-heroism can be demonstrated by comparing Rabbit Angstrom with George Caldwell. Rabbit sees himself as a questing hero and is considered such by some of his contemporaries; in reality, he is a sentimental antihero, a kind of parody of the real thing. On the other hand, George Caldwell is a decent, self-effacing, humble, plodding school teacher, capable of love, sacrifice, duty, and compassion. Like Apollo disguised as Admetus' slave, and like provincial rustics born in stables, Caldwell *is* the genuine hero who frees Prometheus. Rabbit Angstrom, on his nearsighted quest for heroship, becomes a destructive moral anarchist associated with death. George Caldwell, in his plodding daily commitment to duty and work, and in his capacity for love and sacrifice, becomes Chiron, who gives life and freedom to Prometheus. Rabbit Angstrom is a miniscule, scared little animal, a pathetic cipher. George Caldwell is *The Centaur,* the brightest constellation in the heavens.

In *The Centaur* John Updike sings an epic paean and a pastoral lament, and the songs mysteriously emerge as one melody with two sets of words.

6

The Wide-Hipped Wife and the Painted Landscape
Pastoral Ideals in *Of the Farm*

That *The Centaur* (1963) did *not* say the "final word" and bid farewell to Olinger and the farm, as John Updike had intended it to, is made manifest in his writing a type of sequel to *The Centaur*; the sequel is the richly pastoral and anti-pastoral *Of the Farm* (1965). In contrast to the epic-idyllic surrealism of *The Centaur*, *Of the Farm* is relatively realistic, like the earlier Olinger stories of *The Same Door* and *Pigeon Feathers and Other Stories*. However, the novel predictably departs from the Howellsian tradition of realism through two technical devices characteristic of John Updike's fiction: 1) the employment of elaborately extended metaphors and symbols, and 2) the extensive employment of strikingly poetic lyricism. Both the metaphors and the lyricism are directly related to the overall pattern of pastoral and anti-pastoral elements which, as I have indicated, prominently runs through Updike's fiction.

Of the Farm begins with Updike's familiar symbolic actions of "turning off the highway" and "ushering in the land." [1] In terms of literary history, it is the familiar process of turning from the sophisticated Alexandrian court, and entering the idyllic pastures of Arcadia, Sicily, and Syracuse. Or, perhaps more pertinent to this novel, the process of leaving Duke Frederick's Court (New York), fleeing to Arden Forest (the farm), and finally returning to the court—wiser, more reconciled, and mellowed by the disillusioning but clarifying experiences in the rural setting. Like the characters in *As You Like It*, the characters in *Of the Farm* find the bucolic setting full of emotional violence, conflict, and potentially dangerous myths. In several ways *Of the Farm* becomes a parody of the peace and tranquility usually associated with the pastoral existence, in the way Arden Forest, for instance, becomes a parody of Arcady. In using certain linguistic and formal conventions of the pastoral mode (most notably the pastoral love lyric, since the novel is about loving), Updike comments on some fundamental premises of the agrarian myth. To the extent that he uses those techniques partially to expose fallacies in that myth, he creates a work closely akin to the mock-pastoral. In that way, the novel echoes Hawthorne's technique in *The Blithedale Romance*, which is also a novel about sophisticated urbanites who spend a time on a farm.

But the book is much more than an anti-pastoral exposé. In a real way, the farm itself (as the title suggests) is the central subject and the main "character" in the novel. The farm, like the pastures and groves of the Theocritan *Idyls*, is an *idea* as surely as it is a tangible reality—in fact, *more surely* than it is a tangible reality. The farm stands for something different in the minds of each of the four characters in the book: for the old and dying mother, Mrs. Robinson, it is a paradise, a "people sanctuary"; for her middle-aged son Joey, it is a burden imposed by his mother upon him and his father; for Joey's new "broad-hipped" wife, it is an interesting piece of real estate; for Joey's precociously scientistic young stepson, it is a mildly interesting empirical phenomenon. But, in relation to Updike's epigraph for the novel, the significant point is not *what the farm stands for*, but, rather, *that the farm stands*. The book's epigraph is from the existentialist philosopher, Jean Paul Sartre:

Consequently, when, in all honesty, I've recognized that man is a being in whom existence precedes essence, that he is a free being who, in various circumstances, can want only his freedom, I have at the same time recognized that I can want only the freedom of others.

Possibly the best clarification of the ambiguous semantic sophistry involved in the terms *essence* and *existence* is William Barrett's lucidly direct explanation:

The essence of a thing is *what* the thing is; existence refers rather to the sheer fact *that* the thing is. Thus when I say "I am a man," the "I am" denotes the fact that I exist, while the predicate "man" denotes *what kind* of existent I am, namely a man.[2]

Thus, on one level *Of the Farm* is a rather simple "existentialist" commentary saying, "Different realities exist for different people, depending on personal psychology and points of view"—a truism and cliché hardly worth saying. But the latter part of Sartre's epigraph involves the type of tension and conflict on which dramatic fiction can be based; that is, the struggle to recognize and desire "the freedom of others." I take it that such a desire involves love (or is love), and that *Of the Farm* is essentially a book about the relationship between loving and desiring freedom. Furthermore, the theme is a continuation of the treatment of love and freedom in *The Centaur*, where Chiron's sacrificial act of love is directly associated with the attainment of Prometheus' freedom—that is, it ultimately becomes associated with Peter's freedom to become a second-rate abstract painter, if that is what he wants. "The farm" becomes a symbol of that freedom in *Of the Farm*. In the mother's mind, the farm is a kind of pastoral ideal, or paradise; in the son's mind, the farm is curiously associated with the "landscape" of his second wife's sexy body. Both visions employ a degree of imaginative idealizing peculiar to the pastoral manner. The conclusion of the novel shows the son and mother "striking terms" when the son admits, "I've always thought of it as *our* farm."[3] The statement is essentially an act of love and reconciliation which says, "I will give you the freedom to have your 'farm,' and I want to retain my freedom to have my 'farm.'" It is a reenactment of the compassionate father's act of love which had allowed Mrs. Robinson the freedom to have her farm in the first place.

Perhaps the most important fact about *Of the Farm* is that Updike chose the particular image of a farm to symbolize his existential statement about love and freedom. That is, in terms of imagery and language and symbols, characters in the novel become involved in a complex process of pastoral idealization. For example, the boy Richard's question, "What's the point of a farm nobody farms?" [4] indicates that the farm is not "real" in terms of, say, pragmatic agrarian economy. The question is comparable to "what's the point of the Arcadian ideal?" The answer implied throughout the novel is, "The point is the Farm's symbolic value— its value *as an idea*." In choosing to write about "a farm nobody farms," Updike connotatively appeals to all such farms, from Eden to Thoreau's hut at Walden Pond.

Symbolic of Mrs. Robinson's view of the farm is the framed print of a painting which she has hung on the wall to replace the photograph of her son's first wife. That first wife had fallen short of the mother's ideal, and her photograph is replaced by an extravagantly idealized painting of a farm. As in Theocritan *Idyls,* it is "a fabulous rural world" where the grass is "impossibly green." This "idyllic little landscape" suggests the mother's imaginative flight from reality, and her desire for the Arcadian ideal.

In [the portrait's] place above the sofa, not quite filling the tell-tale rectangle of less discolored wallpaper, there had been substituted an idyllic little landscape, a much-reduced print of an oil, that had ornamented my room as a child, when we lived in my grandparents' house in the town. Instantly—and I wanted my mother to see me doing this, as a kind of rebuke—I went to examine the print closely. The pentagonal side of a barn was diagonally bisected by a purple shadow cast by nothing visible, and a leafless tree of uncertain species stood rooted in lush grass impossibly green. Beyond, I revisited, bending deeper into the picture, a marvellous sky of lateral stripes of pastel color where as a child I had imagined myself treading, upside-down, a terrain of crayons. The tiny black V of one flying bird was planted in this sky, between two furrows of color, so that I had imagined that if my fingers could get through the glass they could pluck it up, like a carrot sprout. This quaint picture, windowing a fabulous rural world, had hung, after we had moved to the farmhouse, in the room at the head of the stairs, where I had slept as an adolescent and where, when I had gone away, my father had slept in turn.[5]

This painting is typical of the mother's vision of the world. She creates a pastoral mythology which her son has always seen as contradictory and unrealistic. For example, the son (who narrates the story in the first person) explains that his mother had "made a mythology of her life," a mythology which had a kind of mathematical consistency within its own limits, although it required "feats of warping and circumvention and paradoxical linkage" unintelligible to an outsider.[6] In speaking of the pictures in a nature book owned by his mother, Joey explains to his step-son, "I could never match the pictures up with the real things, exactly. The ideal versus the real."[7] As Mrs. Robinson's ideals and expectations are continually confronted by harsh reality, so her farm is becoming an island encroached upon by superhighways, housing developments, and shopping centers. As part of her ideal, she had wanted her son to be a poet; instead he became an advertising executive. She had never approved of his petite, self-contained, spiritual first wife; neither does she approve of his "wide-hipped," bikini-clad second wife. The mother's problem in loving is that she does not recognize that allowing the loved-one freedom is the first prerequisite. She insists on her private mythology—her painted pastoral landscape. The result is that she has maintained a possessive attitude toward her son which has played a part in the failure of his first marriage. Insofar as Updike shows her particular vision of the world as solipsistic and potentially destructive, the novel is anti-pastoral. But, insofar as he gives her humor, imagination, wit, and even beauty, the novel suggests that there is, after all, something of value in the idealizing pastoral attitude.

The most telling aspect of the novel is the imagery which indicates that Joey, while contemptuous of his mother's idealization and love of the farm, participates in a form of mythologizing very similar to his mother's. As his mother has centered her life around a personal myth about her land, Joey has centered his life around his sexy new wife. He has painfully decided to divorce his first wife, Joan, and lose his three children in order to marry Peggy. And Peggy's great appeal is her voluptuous sexuality—sexuality which he imagines throughout the novel as a *landscape*. In images every bit as ideally pastoral as Mrs. Robinson's "fabulous rural world" in the painting, Joey, as first-person narrator, says of his sexy wife, "she yields a variety of landscapes," and "my wife is a field." In a love lyric as lush and musical as the Theocritan *Idyls* themselves, he celebrates his wife's wide hips and her body:

My wife is wide, wide-hipped and long-waisted, and, surveyed from above, gives an impression of terrain, of a wealth whose ownership imposes upon my own body a sweet strain of extension; entered, she yields a variety of landscapes, seeming now a snowy rolling perspective of bursting cotton bolls seen through the Negro arabesques of a fancywork wrought-iron balcony; now a taut vista of mesas dreaming in the midst of sere and painterly ochre; now a gray French castle complexly fitted to a steep green hill whose terraces imitate turrets; now something like Antarctica; and then a receding valleyland of blacks and purples where an unrippled river flows unseen between shadowy banks of grapes that are never eaten. Over all, like a sky, withdrawn and cool, hangs—hovers, stands, *is*—the sense of her consciousness, of her composure, of a non-committal witnessing that preserves me from claustrophobia through any descent however deep.[8]

For Joey, freedom is associated with his sexy wife, and his sexy wife, in turn, is associated in his mind with the landscape. For his mother, freedom is associated with the landscape of her farm. Indeed, the mother and the son are both idealizing pastoralists. In a review of *Of the Farm* for *Commonweal*, Anthony Burgess comments on the above love lyric as a touch of "genuine pastoral"; he is perhaps the first of Updike's published critics to use the term in connection with Updike's fiction, and, to my knowledge, he is the only one.

There is more of this [lyricism] in the novel, evoking the sexual landscape in the penultimate chapter of *Finnegans Wake*, but totally wideawake, a cunning rococo cadenza or perhaps something earlier and baroque—the fantasy-making extravagance of the metaphysical poets. Sometimes the preciosity is unbearable—"sere and painterly ochre," for example—but on the whole the thing works. It is the sort of thing that brings poetry back to the novel—not the poetry of action or casual close description but the poetry of digression, the only kind really admissible.

Touches like this give *Of the Farm* an intensity, as well as a relaxed quality of genuine "pastoral," very rare in contemporary letters.[9]

My only objection to these incisive comments by Burgess is to question his term "digression," which somehow suggests that such passages are fragmented tours de force, rather than integrated parts of a larger pattern—the pattern I have traced in this essay. Indeed, such lyricism becomes even more attractive and more praiseworthy, it seems to me, when seen in relation to the totality of John Updike's pastoral and anti-pastoral patterns.

Joey's imaginative equation of Peggy's wide-hipped body with the land is further reinforced in the novel. In the way that he sees her body as a landscape while he is making love to her, he conversely sees the landscape as her body while he is mowing the meadow. Complete with a stock pastoral catalogue of flowers, the following idyl shows the process by which Joey becomes sexually aroused as he rides the tractor over the hills and valleys of the meadow:

Black-eyed susans, daisy fleabane, chicory, goldenrod, butter-and-eggs each flower of which was like a tiny dancer leaping, legs together, scudded past the tractor wheels. Stretched scatterings of flowers moved in a piece, like the heavens, constellated by my wheels' revolution, on my right; and lay as drying fodder on my left. Midges existed in stationary clouds that, though agitated by my interruption, did not follow me, but resumed their self-encircling conversation. Crickets sprang crackling away from the wheels; butterflies loped through their tumbling universe and bobbed above the flattened grass as the hands of a mute concubine would examine, flutteringly, the corpse of her giant lover. The sun grew higher. The metal hood acquired a nimbus of heat waves that visually warped each stalk. The tractor body was flecked with foam and I, rocked back and forth on the iron seat shaped like a woman's hips, alone in nature, as hidden under the glaring sky as at midnight, excited by destruction, weightless, discovered in myself a swelling which I idly permitted to stand, thinking of Peggy. My wife is a field.[10]

Mindful that the story is told by a self-revelatory first-person narrator, we must remember that this is Joey Robinson's language, and *his* myth-making; in this lyricism he reveals that he has learned his mother's lessons in pastoralism perhaps better than he himself knows.

The pastoralism of Mrs. Robinson and her son is "genuine." And the novel as a whole would be an idyl, were it not for certain very unpastoral facts and realities brought out in the book; for example, how idyllic are the following details: divorce, three fatherless children, adultery, menstrual periods and soiled Tampax, screaming family fights with slappings and deliberately broken dishes, heart attacks, and an eleven-year-old child caught in the middle of it all? Certainly, there is nothing very extraordinary about these details; they are merely the more unpleasant "stuff of real life." But their very intrusion into Mrs. Robinson's farm is like the intrusion of violence, hypocrisy, and cloddish stupidity into Arden Forest—or, for that matter, like death and communal sin in *The Poorhouse Fair*, or like the ruthless killing in "Pigeon Feathers." Thus, Updike seems to be using the pastoral lyricism of this novel partly as a norm against which reality is measured. The idealized painting and the description of the "wide-hipped wife" serve to remind us and the characters how far we are from Arcady and Eden. In this way, at least, the novel is anti-pastoral.

The most important point made in *Of the Farm* is that all the characters learn something. They partially learn to see things as they are. In the opening paragraph, we see that honeysuckle and poison ivy grow from the same earth and tangle around each other. Similarly ambiguous, the possessiveness of Joey's mother has taught him how to receive Peggy's love; Peggy's earthy voluptuousness is a complement to Joey's poetic mythologizing; Joey's youth on the farm has taught him to love Peggy's earthiness. In short, the characters intuitively grasp what Sartre is talking about in the epigraph—that one must first long for and achieve his *own* freedom before he can love others; and, even then, the first step in loving others is to desire the freedom of the person loved. If "existence precedes essence," then attainment of self-freedom precedes the desire for the freedom of others.

Of the Farm is anti-pastoral without being satiric. At no point in the novel do we see the characters as ridiculous; at no point do we smile or laugh at them, as we sadly smile at Rabbit Angstrom, for example. Even the excessive ideals of the mother and the son have a kind of redemptive eloquence which reminds us more of human aspiration than human folly. In reading this novel, we see that the pastoral ideal has many variations, like a symphony composed around a central theme. For Joey Robinson to metaphorically make his wide-hipped wife into the land is merely an inversion of the process by which Mrs. Robinson makes the land her lover. Both involve the pastoral ideal. The process is ironic without being satiric; and the weekend at the farm is, likewise, parodic without being satiric. The most caustic statement made by *Of the Farm* is that the pastoral attitude toward nature and the land is potentially dangerous. That is, Mrs. Robinson's pastoral idealizing has led to her possessiveness of her son, her inability to accept his spiritual first wife, and her attacks on the new wife Peggy. But Peggy, the very embodiment of earthiness and sexuality, is ironically *like the land*; thus the mother's rejection of Peggy (a conditioned reflex of her possessiveness) is a rejection of her (the mother's) most fundamental beliefs — her own mythology. Consequently, it is bound for failure. Therefore, the stage is set for either some kind of adjustment, or for pathos; and the adjustment occurs. In one of the few scenes of real reconciliation in Updike's fiction, characters adjust: the mother, the new wife, and the son Joey make concessions, and they are concessions which "desire the freedom of others." At the end of the novel, the mother says, "He's a good boy and I've always been tempted to overwork him." In response, "Peggy voluntarily grinned, grinned at me as in my dream or as she had the first time we met." And Joey, freed from his mother's dream of the ideal, concedes the validity of his mother's pastoral dream; that is, he too grants freedom:

" 'Your farm?' I said. 'I've always thought of it as our farm.' " [11] The reconciliation is made valid and is protected from sentimentality by the psychological terror and conflict which have preceded it during the weekend. The "farm" is recognized as existent, and that is sufficient. It no longer matters that Joey's "farm" is his wife, and that the mother's "farm" is the land.

The reconciliation and knowledge which terminates *Of the Farm* are by no means a definitive answer to human conflict. The wisdom attained is like the wisdom so often attained by characters in Shakespeare's plays—a matter of melancholy and faltering reconciliation rather than triumphant affirmation, and a matter of subtle concession rather than dramatic capitulation. Like so much of John Updike's fiction, the novel is concerned with reconciling opposites—farm and town, swain and sophisticate, male and female, spirit and body, past and present, heaven and earth. Here, as in *The Centaur*, the reconciliation occurs. In one sense, *The Centaur* is a pastoral elegy; in a similar sense, *Of the Farm* is a pastoral love lyric. As he had feared, John Updike exaggerated in his desire to make *The Centaur* a valediction to Olinger; if anything, perhaps that distinction belongs more to *Of the Farm* than to any other novel. With only minor exceptions, John Updike has not written anything so hopeful as *Of the Farm* since 1965. And in his most recent works, the "genuine" lyricism and pastoralism of *Of the Farm* have been reduced to painfully ironic norms by which spiritual distance and psychological loss are judged. In his stories collected in *The Music School*, in his novel *Couples*, and in *Bech: A Book* idyllic lyricism is present—but only as an ironic touchstone. To this date, Updike has written nothing so eloquent, so luxurious, and so sanely beneficent as *Of the Farm*.

7

"Fields Still Steeped in Grace"
Idyl and Irony in *The Music School*

In 1966 when I first opened my new edition of *The Music School* collection of short stories and found that John Updike had quoted Wallace Stevens' "To the One of Fictive Music" as the epigraph to the book, I experienced the kind of pleasure one feels when he invites two of his best friends (to his knowledge, strangers to each other) to a party in order that they may get to know each other, only to discover that, unknown to him, they too have been close friends and mutual admirers all along. Wallace Stevens and John Updike share the distinction of being perhaps the most lyrical, and, at the same time, the toughest-minded artists of our time—Stevens is to modern poetry what Updike is to modern prose. They are idyllists and ironists, singers of love songs and chanters of dirges, poets and parodists—mixing "fictive music" with "possum and taters and sop" to arrive at and recreate what Updike has called "the mixed stuff of human existence."

The "one of fictive music" in Wallace Stevens' poem is that powerful and redemptive entity in each man's mind which allows him somehow to deal with the "gross effigy and simulacrum" which the earth becomes as a result of his birth and his mortality. That "One" is the personification of the power of memory and imagination, the poetic Muse; the "fictive music," itself, is memory and imagination, "out of our imperfections wrought." The poem is a hymn of praise and thanksgiving, and it suggests that memory, after all, is more important than the confused disorder of any given moment of sensory immediacy. In *The Music School* stories, John Updike places the memory of an Olinger high school football game on an autumn evening as the first story in the collection. A prose poem, the story "In Football Season" serves as the peaceful idyllic norm against which all the frustration, divorce, anxiety, and alienation found in the rest of the stories are measured. The final story in the collection is "The Hermit," a poignantly ironic parody of the Thoreauvian attempt to return to nature; it ends in madness and violence. The stories of the collection, first published in the *New Yorker* over a period of four years, are placed in the order in which they were written. The progress from "In Football Season" to "The Hermit" suggests the shift in Updike's emphasis—from the genuine lyricism of nostalgic reminiscence to the ironic lyricism of works like "The Hermit," *Couples*, and "The Wait." This growth and change is part of the larger pastoral and anti-pastoral pattern within the body of his work.

"In Football Season" was first published in book form as the *last* story of *Olinger Stories* (1964). Yet it reappears as the *first* story in *The Music School* (1966). That Updike reprints it in *The Music School* is convincing evidence that he is working in terms of a large metaphor about the past and the present, the simple rural world of youth, and the complex urban world of adulthood and middle age. "In Football Season" is directly addressed to the audience (i.e., it begins, "Do *you* remember . . . ?), and it is a piece of "fictive music"—a remembrance of things past.

Do you remember a fragrance girls acquire in autumn? As you walk beside them after school, they tighten their arms about their books and bend their heads forward to give a more flattering attention to your words, and in the little intimate area thus formed, carved into the clear air by an implicit crescent, there is a complex fragrance woven of tobacco, powder, lipstick, rinsed hair, and that perhaps imaginary and certainly elusive scent that wool, whether in the lapels of a jacket or the nap of a sweater, seems to yield when the cloudless fall sky like the blue bell of a vacuum lifts toward itself the glad exhalations of all things. This fragrance, so faint and flirtatious on those after-noon walks through the dry leaves, would be banked a thousand-fold and lie heavy as the perfume of a flower shop on the dark slope of the stadium when, Friday nights, we played football in the city.[1]

The tone is set; the story is a poem; it is the haunting strain of "fictive music," an idyllic memory of nymphs and swains, clear air, cloudless skies, and fragrances made un-bearably sweet by nostalgia and memory, like the sweet-ness of Keats' "unheard melodies" on a Grecian urn. Not really a description of sensory impressions themselves, the passage is a description of the *memory* of sensory im-pressions—like Theocritus remembering the scents and sounds of the pastoral harvest feasts and vintage celebra-tions of his youth. All this is a matter of tone, of imagina-tively evoking lushness and opulence through the relent-less piling up of detail. Strong appeals are made to the olfactory sense, perhaps the one most detached from the process of intellectual objectification—"complex fragrances," and "elusive scents" control the opening paragraph of the story, and perfume the whole work. The smells of the young people and the Olinger night were "more vivid than that of a meadow," and they eventually become "a concentrated homage, an incense, of cosmetics, cigarette smoke, warmed wool, hot dogs, and the tang, both animal and metallic, of clean hair."[2] Like the original idyls, this idyl is almost religiously celebratory in tone and attitude; indeed, befitting a hymn or religious rite, the odors be-come "incense": "In a hoarse olfactory shout, these odors ascended." The story is reminiscent of Theocritus' "Idyl 7," the pastoral harvest hymn to Demeter (Ceres), which is as much a nostalgic celebration of the swain Lycidas as it is a celebration of the goddess. Also a nostalgic remem-brance of innocent youth, peace, and joy in autumn, the Greek *Idyl* captures the tone of wealth and well-being which marks Updike's story.

There we reclined on deep beds of fragrant lentisk, lowly strown, and rejoicing we lay in new stript leaves of the vine. And high above our heads waved many a poplar, many an elm tree, while close at hand the sacred water from the nymphs' own cave welled forth with murmurs musical. On shadowy boughs the burnt cicadas kept their chattering toil, far off the little owl cried in the thick thorn brake, the larks and finches were singing, the ring-dove moaned, the yellow bees were flitting about the springs. All breathed the scent of the opulent summer, of the season of fruits; pears at our feet and apples by our side were rolling plentiful, the tender branches, with wild plums laden, were earthward bowed, and the four-year-old pitch seal was loosened from the mouth of the wine-jars.[3]

In addition to incense, Updike goes so far as to include a version of a hymn within the idyllic "In Football Season." It is a group song about "getting to heaven," a nonsense song of the type adolescents sing on buses and in social groups—a kind of primitive chorale with leader and chorus. "Oh, you can't get to Heaven/ In a rocking chair . . . !" The song, says the narrator, was "a song for eternity"; closer to a jubilant "Pan's shout" of sheer joy than to formal music, the improvisations provided the musical accompaniment to the teen-agers' walk from the stadium to their homes. "Heroism" on these walks is so simple a thing as the sophomore Billy Trupp's determination to walk home with the group even though he is on crutches because of a broken ankle received in football practice. Reckless "wickedness" at this age of sixteen is as simple as mentioning a motel bed in the lyrics of the group song. Sexual excitement and involvement is limited to walking a girl to her door and kissing her good night. And Olinger, enchanted by youth and autumn, is "like a town in a fable" [4]—or like the setting of a pastoral idyl:

The hour or more behind me, which I had spent so wastefully, in walking when a trolley would have been swifter, and so wickedly, in blasphemy and lust, was past and forgiven me; it had been necessary; it was permitted.[5]

The last paragraph of "In Football Season" suggests that youth is a period of grace—when innocent "sin" curiously contains its own built-in redemption and forgiveness. The fragrance of young girls comes from the fact that they are *"carrying invisible bouquets from fields still steeped in grace*"—that is, from their very youth, innocence, and joy in being alive. Those "fields still steeped in grace" are the archetypal fields of Arcady and Hybla; and Joanne Hardt, Nanette Seifert, Henny Gring, and Leo Horst are counterparts of Amaryllis, Galatea, Lycidas, and Thyrsis. But the narrator of "In Football Season" has lost that world through the passage of time and through awareness of his own mortality. For him, the fragrance of young girls evokes the same response as the passage of a hearse: they remind him of his loss of innocence and his mortality, as surely as the thought of Eden is accompanied by the concomitant thought of man's fall from grace. The two go together. The last paragraph of the lyrical idyl sets the key for the rest of the stories in *The Music School* collection:

Now I peek into windows and open doors and do not find that air of permission. It has fled the world. Girls walk by me carrying their invisible bouquets from fields still steeped in grace, and I look up in the manner of one who follows with his eyes the passage of a hearse, and remembers what pierces him.[6]

The rest of the stories in the collection are about characters who have lost their youth and innocence—from the adulterous neurotic narrator of "The Music School" to the quarreling couple in "Twin Beds in Rome." The characters in these stories are sophisticates who vacation in France, Rome, Charlotte Amalie. They measure their unhappiness by remembrance of earlier days—by the "fictive music" of memory. In "The Music School," the middle-aged narrator vaguely perceives some relationship between 1) a recent discussion about receiving the Eucharist, 2) the recent murder of an acquaintance, and 3) his young daughter's piano lessons in the basement of a Baptist church. He also feels that these phenomena are vaguely tied up with the failure of his marriage. The murdered acquaintance was a computers expert, a totally intellectualized and mechanized modern man—strangely like the computers themselves. As in the last sentence of "In Football Season," the narrator, a novelist, uses the word *pierce* to explain the pain of his existence: His daughter's "pleased

smile . . . pierces [his] heart." [7] The pain is characteristic of a type found throughout Updike's fiction. It is the
pain of the sophisticate longing for his swainship in Olinger.
Religious faith and hopefulness stamped those innocent
days, and remembrance of them is more painful than con-
soling. The adultery and promiscuity which become an important theme in the stories of *The Music School* and in
Couples are symbolic of attempts to recapture the innocence and "permissiveness" of youthful sexuality. Updike's
later heroes, like the earlier Rabbit Angstrom, are unable to age, and they make Rabbit's mistake of trying to
replace an idyllic ideal with a physical reality. At the end of
"The Music School," it is the daughter's refreshing youth
which pierces her father's heart, because he is reminded of
his loss and distance from that youth:

> The world is the host; it must be chewed. I am content here
> in this school. My daughter emerges from her lesson. Her face is
> fat and satisfied, refreshed, hopeful; her pleased smile, biting her
> lower lip, pierces my heart, and I die (I think I am dying) at
> her feet. [8]

The daughter is "still steeped in grace," and her father's
pain is the pain of Adam as he looked back toward Eden.
Updike, in associating youth with hearses and death,
becomes aligned with the Romanticism of poets like John
Keats, who knew that pastoral scenes on Grecian urns were
melancholy paradoxes, with nymphs and swains and music
on one side, and a ceremonial death processional on the
other. On one side, the adolescents of "In Football Season"; on the other, as the natural and inescapable complement, the "passage of a hearse." Keats's "ditties of no tone"
are themselves "fictive music," which does not pipe to the
sensual ear, but to the spirit. The narrators of "In Football
Season" and "The Music School" are the precursors of the
carefully developed character, Piet Hanema, of *Couples*.
These characters are superannuated sensitive young swains,
adulterous, nostalgically religious, and preoccupied with
death. And in attempting to recapture the pastoral ideal
through illicit sex, they become destructive and life-denying.

The last two stories in *The Music School* collection are ironic pastorals, in which the entire American tradition of agrarianism and return to nature are revealed as lost ideals, freakish and absurd parodies of 1) the old-fashioned family reunion in a meadow, and 2) the Thoreauvian hut in the woods. "The Family Meadow" and "The Hermit" both clearly show the direction which Updike's idyllic lyricism has taken in his later works.

"The Family Meadow" opens with a description of the site of the family reunion:

> The family always reconvenes in the meadow. For generations it has been traditional, this particular New Jersey meadow, with its great walnut tree making shade for the tables and its slow little creek where the children can push themselves about in a rowboat and nibble watercress and pretend to fish.[9]

Old and young, the family reunite at this pleasant rural spot. They pitch horseshoes, eat, and talk in the midsummer heat. It would seem to be a version of an idyl, were it not for the unexpected fact which we learn at the end of the story. The land on three sides of the meadow has given way to suburban ranch houses, the creek is polluted, and the family meadow has become "like a zoo" to the residents of the housing development.[10] The irony is that the family cling to an idea which is no longer tenable, even though it is strongly attractive. The discrepancy between the meadow and the shoddy housing development is an indictment of the development rather than the pastoral ideal. But the central point is that the anti-pastoral forces—that is, forces which oppose the pastoral attitude and ideal—are potently inexorable. And, at best, the family reunion is a self-conscious parody of its earlier original, in the way the courtships and sexual adventures in *Couples* are, at best, parodies of youthful, adolescent sexual experiences.

In "The Hermit," the last story in *The Music School*, a middle-aged janitor attempts to retreat to the freedom and simplicity of a hut in the woods. He fails for the same reason Rabbit Angstrom had failed in *his* attempt to return to nature: he lacks the sophistication to realize that an

imaginative escape and a physical escape are not synony-
mous and interchangeable. In other words, he does not
understand the premise behind all idyls—the fundamental
fact that Olinger or Walden or Arcady is a "state of mind"
rather than a physical location. The result is that Stanley's
life as a hermit in the woods is a pathetic parody of the
Thoreauvian experience at Walden. Whereas Thoreau's hut
was a symbolically purified house of the mind, Stanley's
hut is one room of a deserted old farmhouse; whereas
Thoreau read Homer, Stanley reads badly written nine-
teenth-century fiction and biography; whereas Thoreau
bathed in the cold purity of depthless Walden Pond, Stanley
bathes in a tiny rivulet too shallow to cover his body;
whereas Thoreau's stay in the woods led to philosophical
affirmation of the universe, Stanley's stay leads to madness.
The details of the story are curiously parallel to the details
of *Walden*, with the exception that they are pitifully reduced to absurd echoes of the Thoreauvian experience.
The dream of shedding one's clothes and mystically com-
muning with nature is interpreted as an act of madness in
the twentieth century. Stanley *does* achieve a mystical
union with nature in the story, but the union necessarily
separates him from humanity. And characters who set themselves apart from the sinfulness and imperfection of all
other humans are bound for anguish and failure in Updike's fiction. The dream of paradise and harmony with
nature, attractive as it may be, is depicted as a type of
destructive pride.

The hermit is on a quest; and his goal is the innocence
and simplicity of Nature itself. He sets up his forest home
in April, and he reaches a psychological climax in May, the
pastoral month; his perceptions of natural growth and
rhythm become acutely heightened.[11]

His total commitment to nature involves icy Thoreauvian baths. But his ritualistic baths are ironic reductions of
those described by Thoreau in *Walden* and by Walt Whitman in *Specimen Days*.

The stream was only inches deep and a man's width wide; to
wet himself Stanley had to lie on the bed of red sand and
smoothed sandstones and make of himself a larger stone that the

little stream, fumbling at first, icily consented to lave. To wet his back he would roll over and lie staring up at the explosive blue rents in the canopy of leaves, like a drowning man frozen during his final glimpse of sky. Then he would rise, dripping, a silver man, and walk naked back, slightly uphill, through the warm ragged mulch of last autumn's leaves.[12]

It is after one of these baths that he is surprised by a young boy from the town. The boy becomes frightened, and Stanley runs after him to reassure him.

The boy was the first to speak. "I'm sorry," he said, and turned to run, and Stanley, seized by an abrupt fear of loss, of being misunderstood, ran after him—a terrifying figure, probably, gaunt and wet and wordlessly openmouthed among the serene verticals of the trees, his penis a-bobble.[13]

Stanley's brothers and townsmen come to capture him, to remove him from his hermitage, and the idyl ends in a violent constriction—"a bumbling, a thumping, a clumsy crushing clamor."[14] The scene and the story is reminiscent of all conflicts between pastoralists and anti-pastoralists, with the confrontation between the Merry Mount maypolers and the practical Plymouth Puritans serving as a kind of American prototype. The earliest literature written in America includes a similar conflict. Stanley is unaware that he is following a basic direction of the American dream; nor are the anti-pastoralist intruders aware of their Puritan predecessors. But the patterns are there. The reader sympathizes with Stanley even as he realizes that the hermit is fated; and he realizes that, pragmatically and numerically, the anti-pastoralists will prevail.

"The Hermit" must be seen in historical terms. But it is also important in psychological terms. For example, Updike makes the "sane" brothers and townsmen far less sympathetic than the hermit. He affirms Emily Dickinson's observation that "much madness is divinest sense to a discerning eye." Still, we are unable to accept Stanley's quest as a valid solution to the complexities of modern existence. Stanley and Rabbit Angstrom "run" to the woods for refuge; but in alienating themselves from human bonds (neither, for example, is able to establish stable relationships with women), they merely become further estranged and more anguished. To the extent that the quests of characters such as Rabbit Angstrom, Stanley, and Piet Hanema are shown as types of folly and exaggeration, we can perceive something like a satiric wink from Updike. But it is the kindest type of satire, more like the didacticism of moral fable than anything else. Certainly, the backward longing for pastoral "fields of grace" is potentially destructive, as manifested by its symbolic linkage with death and madness in Updike's fiction. But that longing becomes part of each reader's own "fictive music" as he realizes, with the melancholy and frustration that always accompany wisdom, that he too has suffered the loss of Paradise. Updike's progress from an idyllist to an ironist is, technically and thematically, a sign of maturity and growth; and the stories of *The Music School* illuminate the fundamental patterns of his fiction perhaps as well as anything else he has written.

8

The Tarbox "Nymphs and Satyrs"
Couples as a Didactic Anti-Pastoral

John Updike has said of *Couples* (Knopf, 1968), "All these goings-on would be purely lyrical, like nymphs and satyrs in a grove, except for the group of distressed and neglected children." [1] Whatever else *Couples* may or may not be, it is part of the elaborate myth and metaphor which constitutes an overall pattern of pastoralism and anti-pastoralism in Updike's fiction. And the pastoralism and lyricism of this novel are cuttingly ironic—like the drawing on the dust jacket. The drawing is William Blake's water-color, "Adam and Eve Sleeping." It is a luxuriant portrayal of our first parents languorously asleep in the lush vegetation of pre-lapsarian Eden. Young and perfect, they sleep the dreamless sleep of uncorrupted innocence, guarded by two hovering angels. But the disturbing elements of the drawing are a waning moon in the background, and a fat, bug-eyed toad in the foreground, inches away from Eve's face. The lyricism of the drawing is made ironic and set in a minor key by these anti-pastoral elements. And we know that this first "couple" will awaken to enact the terrible motions which will plunge them and the race into sin, death, and corruption. The novel within these covers concerns the entanglements of middle-aged twentieth-century couples who attempt to return to their youth and innocence by 1) moving to pastoral Tarbox, Massachusetts, and 2) becoming involved in sexual adventures as if they were adolescent nymphs and swains.

Their follies, their excesses, and their pastoral visions have destructive results. However, these excesses and this vision have been a part of the American Dream from the time of the earliest American settlements, and the flight to pastoral Tarbox is a version of Thomas Morton's flight from England to Merry Mount, where "duty and work yielded as ideals to truth and fun." [2] "Duty and work" are Puritan ideals, those of William Bradford's Plymouth settlers, whereas "frisking and worse" are associated with the Merry Mount tradition. In *Couples*, the "Applesmiths" were reared in highly sophisticated urban homes—country club atmospheres of great wealth, great formality, and great complexity. In fleeing to Tarbox, the Applebys and the Little Smiths consciously seek the pastoral escape to rural simplicity.

They put behind them the stratified summer towns of their upbringings, with their restrictive distinctions, their tedious rounds of politeness, and settled the year round in unthought-of places, in pastoral mill towns like Tarbox, and tried to improvise here a fresh way of life. Duty and work yielded as ideals to truth and fun. Virtue was no longer sought in temple or market place but in the home—one's own home, and then the homes of one's friends.[3]

In the novel, duty and work are abandoned on such a large and exaggerated scale that they are no longer major concerns to the characters. The two epigraphs for the novel, from Paul Tillich's *The Future of Religions* and Alexander Blok's "The Scythians," suggest that the novel has some kind of didactic statement to make about social responsibility. Tillich says that to believe that one's personal life does not concern "the life of the society to which he belongs" is "unfavorable for the preservation of a living democracy." But the deterministic and apathetic social attitude *does* ironically produce a "mood favorable for the resurgence of religion." In *Couples* the hedonistic abandon with which promiscuous sexuality is embraced has the earmarks of religious fervor; but, of course, maypole frolics and bacchanals are types of religious ceremonies by their very nature. Priapian and Eleusinian cults rank among the oldest of the world's religions. The lines from "The Scythians" suggest

that lovers and worshippers of the flesh become lovers of
death also; and barbaric sensualists ask, "Are we to blame
if your fragile bones/ Should crack beneath our heavy, gentle paws?" In short, the epigraphs show solipsistic hedonists
as fatalistic determinists—and the novel shows the consequences of such thinking.

The question arises as to whether *Couples* is straight
moral didacticism, or satirical didacticism. Despite Updike's
demurrer that the novel is "critical" rather than "satiric,"
it seems to me that the novel is partially satiric, in the way
Rabbit, Run is partially satiric.[4] That is, the absurdity and
the sustained exaggeration of the novel (along with names
of characters and places, ironic lyricism, and parodic stereo-
typing) require that the novel be read as satire. And to miss
the satiric point is to miss much of the novel—like those reviewers, for example, who found the novel merely pornographic.[5] Again in this novel, Updike refuses to make the
novel either wholly comic and satiric or wholly serious and
pathetic. In using a technique which includes both satire
and straight didacticism, he seems to have puzzled his readers who want either to laugh *or* to cry—but not both. These
readers are like moviegoers who didn't know how to respond
to movies such as *Bonnie and Clyde* and Truffaut's *Jules et
Jim.* That we sympathize with Rabbit Angstrom and Piet
Hanema does not mean we cannot smile at and condemn
their excesses; that their quests are so close to our own and
that we are so much like them does not mean that we
should overlook their ridiculousness. If the standard for
satire can be reduced to the question "Is some ridicule intended?", then *Couples* is satiric. Certainly, to the extent
that widespread notions of pastoral and agrarian ideals exist as part of the American Dream, and to the extent that
the goings-on in Tarbox are parodic exaggerations and contradictions of those ideals, the novel is satiric.

Couples deals with two of John Updike's "Great Secret
Things": religion and sex. If the novel has a central character, it is Piet Hanema, who is married to Angela. His
name suggests "piety," "amen," and, as Freddy Thorne suggests, "enema." His aloof and self-contained wife is, of

course, an "angel." Piet is a version of a standard Updike character—the sensitive pastoral swain who has lost his youth and his faith, and who goes on a quest to find them. As in Rabbit Angstrom's case, religion and sex become intertwined in this quest. And the quest is directly related to some type of pastoral or agrarian ideal. For example, Piet's background is directly related to pastoralism: his parents had run a greenhouse, he had grown up with a strong protestant religious faith, he had experienced the poignant adolescent sexual initiation with the nymph Anabelle Vojt, and he has been removed from all this through age and spatial distance. All of these details become norms by which Piet judges his present life. His very dreams become journeys back into the pastoral past. He thinks of sex in lyrical, idyllic terms: He dreams of his high school nymph, Annabelle Vojt, as he lies beside his sleeping wife. Consciously and unconsciously, he rejects his present and returns to an earlier idyllic past.

In church, pastoral shepherds are associated with religion:

Piet had been raised in a sterner church, the Dutch Reformed, amid varnished oak and dour stained glass where shepherds were paralyzed in webs of lead.[6]

And of the two ushers sitting in a pew in front of him, "one of them had *satyr's ears*, the holes tamped with wiry hair." Piet's parents had been killed in a car wreck while "driving home to Grand Rapids *from a Grange meeting*." His father is described as a "placid good gardener."

Tarbox itself is built around a pastoral village green, and the church is built upon what was once "common pasturage." The town was built along "wobbly pasture lanes, quaintly named for the virtues, that radiated from the green."[7] The Countryside, apart from the creeping, anti-pastoral new developments, is idyllic,

. . . the new developments like even pastel teeth eating the woods of faraway Indian Hill. Beyond, there was a veiny weave of roads, an arrowing disused railroad track, a river whose water was fresh above the yellow water-fall at the factory and saline below it, a golf course studded with bean-shapes of sand, some stubborn farms and checkerboard orchards, a glinting dairy barn on the Nun's Bay Road, a field containing slowly moving specks that were galloping horses, level breadths of salt marsh broken by islands and inlets, and, its curved horizon marred, on days as clear as today, by the violet smudge that was the tip of Cape Cod, the eastward sea.[8]

The community is referred to as "the post-pill paradise," [9] a community as Edenic and paradisaical as the settings of Theocritan *Idyls*. It is a modern version of "The New English Canaan."

Piet's first adulterous tryst is graphically described in lyrical terms. He and Georgene Thorne copulate on the sun-roof "beneath the span of sky and treetops and birdsong, which he truly loved." Like pastoral nymph and satyr, "they lay together beneath the whispering trees, Hansel and Gretel abandoned. Shed needles from the larches had collected in streaks and puddles on the tarpaper and formed rusty ochre drifts along the wooden balustrade." [10] One recalls Updike's earlier references to making love on beds of pine needles under the trees. Their sex is described in liltingly lyrical tones:

A cloud passingly blotted the sun. Sensing and fearing a witness, Piet looked upward and was awed as if by something inexplicable, by the unperturbed onward motion of the fleet of blue-bellied clouds, ships with a single destination. The little eclipsing cloud burned gold in its tendrilous masts and stern. A cannon discharge of irridescence, and it passed. Passed on safely above him. Sun was renewed in bold shafts on the cracked April earth, the sodden autumnal leaves, the new shoots coral in the birches and mustard on the larch boughs, the dropped needles drying, the tarpaper, their discarded clothes. Between her breasts the sweat was scintillant and salt.[11]

The lyricism is ironic because the lovers are middle-aged parents of children rather than young nymphs and swains. The reference to Hansel and Gretel suggests that the lovers are involved in a fairy tale of their own making. Their adultery is largely a matter of sexual convenience in which their emotions are excluded. And this incident is merely one of many within the novel; finally, all but four of the twenty individuals among the "couples" commit or consider adultery (of the four who don't, one is dying, one is an emotionless automaton, and two are practicing Roman Catholics). The very exaggeration of the act suggests a satirical treatment; fully sixteen of the twenty people involved are neither strong enough nor virtuous enough to avoid adulterous entanglement.

Other pastoral elements exist in the novel. When Marcia Smith and Frank Appleby first commit adultery, they choose a resort cottage in the woods north of Boston: "The cottage was used only on weekends. From its security amid pines and pin oaks it overlooked the slender peninsula of Nahant." Afterward, Marcia feels compelled to be more free with her husband; they begin going for nude swims together —like a naked Adam and Eve. It is finally the Smiths and the Applebys who flatly trade wives and husbands with each other. They long for innocence and simplicity; their attempts to find them through uninhibited sexuality bring frustration and complexity.

Too many of these lyrical passages exist to cite them all; the elements of pastoralism and the desire for innocence are dominant throughout the novel. The important fact about the couples' attempts is that none of them really succeeds. Piet's affair with Foxy ends in divorce and abortion. Piet and his children are preoccupied with death in the novel; the implication is that hedonism is eventually life-denying, as the epigraph from "The Scythians" suggests. Piet and Foxy do finally get married at the end of the novel, and they move away to start life over in a new town. But they have become involved with a new set of "couples." Piet is perhaps no worse than the rest of the couples, and he certainly feels he is better. The fact remains that he causes pain for his own children and death for Foxy's unborn child. The novel is an indictment of the entire Tarbox way of life, and as such, it is an indictment of pastoralism itself.

Couples is clearly didactic, and one of the things it seems to be saying is that the romantic quest for the idyllic life in nature is dangerous to both individuals and to society as a whole. It is the same conclusion which William Bradford and John Endicott drew in regard to the original American pastoralists—the Merry Mount maypolers. And it is the same thing Nathaniel Hawthorne tried to show in *The Blithedale Romance* and "The Maypole of Merry Mount." It is what Sinclair Lewis showed in Babbitt's dream of "The Fairy Child" and in Babbitt's attempt to flee to the Maine woods. *Couples* may well be the most moral novel written in the twentieth century. Updike believes that human beings *can* make choices; his anti-pastoral fiction is designed largely to show that romantic pastoralism and unrealistic idealism are dangerous choices.

The myth of the fall of man from grace is not merely an historical concept within Updike's fiction. Rather, *each individual* reenacts the old pattern during his own lifetime. Youth and adolescence are the times of Edenic grace; then, each man falls. The Hebraic-Christian tradition teaches that man can never retain his state of innocence; on the contrary, like Updike's one genuine hero, the Centaur, he must work and love within the limits of his corrupted state, and hope for redemption. Updike's gallery of questing anti-heroes refuses to accept those fundamental limitations of man's condition. And in their desire to regain paradise here on earth, they damn their souls. Albert Camus's picture of modern man is the picture of Sisyphus, condemned to an everlasting labor of rolling a great stone up a mountain, only to have it roll down again when he gets to the top. Then he must walk down and start the task again—for eternity. The pastoralist would sit down in the shade at the foot of the mountain and let the grass grow around the rock while he sported with the nymphs in the shadowy grove. That seems to be what the characters of *Couples* would like to do; but if man has any single inexorable fate, it is that he can never return to Eden. What he makes of a fallen world is largely a matter of choice—so long as he realizes he cannot make it into Eden or Arcady. And that seems to be the critical and didactic purpose behind John Updike's elaborate treatment of pastoral and anti-pastoral patterns within *Couples* and within the body of his fiction.

9

Moral Landscape in *Bech: A Book*

Part of the "silken mechanism whereby America reduces her writers to imbecility and cozenage" involves the well-oiled and slippery critical machinery of labeling, categorizing, and pigeonholing them.[1] At its worst, the machinery approximates those uncanny computerized letter-sorting machines which scrutinize envelopes for telltale zip codes, and then, with electronic precision and objectivity, speed the letters through frictionless rollers and bearings to be ejected into neat stacks in the right slots. For literary sorters, the current indispensable and fashionable stacks are strangely sociological, religious, and ethnic, rather than formal, generic, and aesthetic: Malamud, Bellow, and Roth belong in the "Jewish stack;" Ellison, Wright, and Baldwin are "Black novelists;" Updike is a "WASP." The categories are reductive, mindless, and useless; as a rule, they tell little about the writers, and less about their fiction.

Henry Bech, the Manhattan-based Jewish hero of *Bech: A Book* (Knopf, 1970), is as far removed from the Olinger swains of Updike's early fiction as New York City is removed from Shillington, Pennsylvania; or as far as ancient Alexandria was removed from Arcadian Greece. Therefore, the immediate response to the Bech stories is that Updike is deliberately and impishly throwing a monkey wrench into that "silken critical machinery" which has mindlessly reduced him to a WASP chronicler of middle-class American life. Since Norman Mailer first popularized the term "WASP," it has frequently been applied to John Updike, complete with its unfortunate perjorative connotations. And Updike has ironically responded by creating Henry Bech, one of his most sympathetic heroes. Indeed, a satirically vindicative motive may be part of the background of the collection of stories, but it is a minor part. Far more significant is the light which *Bech* sheds on the continuous growth, craftsmanship, and depth of Updike's themes and techniques within the total body of his art.

Writing a collection of stories about a burnt-out Jewish author as his first major work since *Couples* is peculiarly consistent with Updike's penchant for doing the unexpected. One need only recall that twenty-six-year-old Updike created a ninety-four-year-old hero for his first novel, that marital disorder became his theme after the conciliatory *Of the Farm*, and that he has tended to move from the position of a serious pastoralist to that of a satiric antipastoralist in the body of his fiction.

If John Updike's art is characterized by any single trait, it is expansive growth. Updike does leave old themes to go on to new ones. He does finally "say the final word and farewell" to Olinger; [2] he does show that swains grow middleaged and sated in Tarbox; he does reverse his vision to see the United States from Jewish Manhattan, and the land is both "a huge and beautiful wilderness" and "swept by dust storms and storms of Christian conscience." [3] In its imaginative departure from Updike's previous books, *Bech* dramatically reveals Updike's subtle talent as an artist and "maker" in the Aristotelian sense.

Henry Bech's character is rich and complex in itself; he is a sophisticated naïf, a world traveler, a minor celebrity, a soul-searching seeker, a self-caricature. But in relation to the pastoral and anti-pastoral pattern, Bech becomes especially important. For one thing, Henry Bech proves the far-reaching extent to which twentieth-century man longs for a return to nature and innocence. Updike pointedly places Bech in settings and situations where his urbanity and sophistry are juxtaposed against simplicity and naturalness: Russia is a place where there is little to buy except wooden toys and fur pelts; in Rumania, racy underground enter-

tainment is a series of childlike circus acts; Bulgaria pro-
duces peasants, pears for breakfast, fairy tale ballets, and an
exquisite but unapproachable poetess who is like "a motionless white horse silhouetted against a green meadow, pinned
there like a brooch." [4] "Bech Takes Pot Luck" is set in a
rented rural cottage on a dirt road on a Massachusetts island, where Bech's rival is a young boy "connected to the
land in a way Bech could only envy." In "Bech Panics,"
Bech's existential spiritual crisis occurs in a "secluded patch
of oaks" where Bech throws himself on the "woodland's
floor of mulching leaves" to beg "Someone, Something, for
mercy." [5] In "Bech Swings," William Wordsworth's pastoral daffodils bloom in London rains as Bech is exploited
by a gossip columnist and a literary interviewer. And finally, the heaven Bech enters in the final story is peopled by
sadly childlike and dessicated relics of mediocre artists he
had once seen lionized in his own childhood.

To what end does Henry Bech move from green meadows
of Bulgarian valleys to "pantheistic pangs" in oak groves on
a Virginia girls' school campus? In one sense he is an Alexandrian courtier discovering Arcady. Once again in these
stories, evocation of pastoral elements becomes a norm or
touchstone against which sophisticated life is contrasted,
and the result is an ironic devaluation of the seemingly
superior sophistication. The Bech stories are ironic reversals
of the process by which the innocent rural swain comes to
the city to be corrupted by sophistication, as in early Updike stories like "A Gift from the City." In *Bech*, the urban
sophisticate moves toward simplicity and nature (the Iron
Curtain countries are curiously and consistently presented
as childlike and naïve), only to find his sophistication non-
functional and debilitating in those "simpler" worlds. For
example, Henry Bech chronically misreads cues and misin-
terprets gestures in these stories: in "Rich in Russia," he
fails to realize he was supposed to sleep with his female
interpreter; in "Bech Takes Pot Luck," he is convinced that
his ex-student has left the cottage to have sex with Bech's
mistress, whereas the boy has really gone to fetch a manus-
cript for Bech to read, and to flush his LSD down the toilet;

in "Bech Panics," his mystical union with God in the woods is, in truth, a momentary, anticlimactic emotional orgy. And entering heaven is, like the dream of "heaven on earth" in *The Poorhouse Fair*, anticlimax epitomized.

In short, Henry Bech is too sophisticated for his own good, and the satire and comedy of the stories stem from the failure which results when Bech insists on imposing his sophistry on basically unsophisticated situations. It is a subtle variant of the agrarian swain's imposition of his rural values on a complex urban situation, as in "A Gift from the City." [6]

"The Bulgarian Poetess," first collected in *The Music School* (1966), is a small masterpiece of craftsmanship and subtlety. Technically, its skill and control remind one of those Vermeer paintings so greatly admired by Peter-Prometheus in *The Centaur*. Visually, the surfaces, the lighting, the lyricism and precision are Vermeer's, as in the line, "What he had not expected was her appearance here, in this remote and abused nation, in this room of morning light, where he discovered a small knife in his fingers and on the table before him, golden and moist, a precisely divided pear." [7] Objects and surfaces in the story are captured with painterly boldness and imagistic clarity, as in the Theocritan description of the Bulgarian countryside:

An aimless soft rain was falling in these mountains, and there were not many German tourists today. Across the valley, whose little silver river still turned a water wheel, a motionless white horse stood silhouetted against a green meadow, pinned there like a brooch. [8]

The result evokes enchantment and magic—the prevailing tone of the story.

This enchanted other-worldliness is emphasized in several ways. For example, Bech visits a deserted monastery, views a fairy tale ballet entitled *Silver Slippers*, and associates the poetess with a healthy peasant woman and the white horse in the meadow. Indeed, a certain distance in time is evoked by the word *poetess*, which is anachronistic and romantic, like *sorceress* or *empress*. The literary allusions—Bech reads Hawthorne in his hotel room, he meets the translator of

Alice in Wonderland, and Mark Twain and Sinclair Lewis
are discussed—all suggest a romantic or childlike or simple
world of magic and enchantment. The poetess herself is
described as "very feminine, perhaps shallow." Although
Bech admits that "shallowness can be a kind of honesty,"
he is finally unable either to accept or genuinely appreciate
all this magic simplicity.

Bech's problem in "The Bulgarian Poetess" is that he
cannot love. Vera Glavanakova is as distant and unapproachable for Bech as the princess in the ballet, and as
desirable. Her simplicity is her charm (like the feminine
symmetry of the egg imagery of her "ova" name, the oval
mirror in the ballet, and that "precisely divided pear.")

In pastoral terms, Bech's problem is not so much that he
has lost an enchanted Arcadian youth, as it is that his urbanity and sophistication prevent his dealing with it when
he does discover it. Bech's pathetically melodramatic
drunken note which ends the story stands out in stilted
contrast to Vera's charmingly misspelled and candid expression of affection in her note to him. The reader rightly sus-
pects that Bech has gone too far in ordering his own life,
as he has ordered the lives of characters in his fiction; subsequent stories in the book substantiate this suspicion.

The boy in "Bech Takes Pot Luck" is a type of pastoral
swain, whose enviable skills are associated with simple ac-
tivities of the outdoors. Obnoxious and fatuous, still "he was
connected to the land in a way Bech could only envy."
Like the women Bech meets behind the Iron Curtain, and
like the girls at the Virginia college, the boy is connected
to a pastoral world which Bech cannot deal with.

Bech's religious crisis in "Bech Panics" is also connected
with a pastoral landscape, complete with the signposts of a
Theocritan catalogue and an Emersonian "transparent eye-
ball." Bech's "dead eyes, cleansed of healthy egotism, discovered a startled tenderness, like a virgin's whisper, in
every twig, cloud, brick, pebble, shoe, ankle, window mul-
lion, and bottle-glass tint of distant hill." [9]

The entire landscape of the college, with its manure-
fertilized lawns and its secluded oak grove, becomes moral

for Bech. It is the pastoral norm by which he perceives his distance from nature. He tries the transcendental escape to nature, but it does not work. At the end of the story, Bech is merely left hollow, with less identity left than he had before he flung himself on the ground and prayed. The satire is of the type found in *Babbitt*, where the hero seeks freedom in the Maine woods; and it is like the parody of the Thoreauvian escape in Updike's "The Hermit." The difference here is that Henry Bech, like Rabbit Angstrom, is defeated by his own sensibility—the monumental ego which is unable to unite with anything. In these stories *Bech* cannot even unite with a woman through love, much less unite with God through nature.

Finally, Bech is damned by his distance from simplicity and nature. One recalls the way in which pastoral norms exist in Bernard Malamud's fiction—the breezes, hills, and meadows which ironically haunt Morris Bober in *The Assistant*, for example. In Malamud's fiction as in Bech, they are painful reminders of what has been lost, or has never been found.

In "Bech Enters Heaven," we find that traditional agrarianism and transcendentalism have been as foreign to New York-reared Bech as his Judaic religious ceremonies in overheated back rooms are foreign to midwestern protestant America. But Bech's flaw is not that he happens to be urban or Jewish; rather it is that he has believed in the American dream of attaining heaven on earth.

Heaven on earth. Membership in the National Academy of Arts and Sciences? Bech has believed this myth, this concept of a paradise on earth, in the way that the United States as a whole had believed what it had seen in Hollywood movies. Bech has been tricked by a false ideal, and he has "entered heaven" through sacrificing his selfhood and his ability to love.

Bech: A Book stands at what Updike has described as the "Midpoint" in Updike's life.[10] It rounds off the first half of Updike's literary accomplishment, and one can justifiably wait with great expectation for the second half. From pastoral Olinger to anti-pastoral Manhattan, Updike delves into the most fundamental themes and issues of modern American life with sustained craftsmanship and artistry. His penetrating vision equals his poetic gifts of language, and he emerges as one of the most important artists of his time.

Notes

1 – The Pastoral and Anti-Pastoral Modes

1. John Updike, "The Wait," *New Yorker*, February 17, 1968, p. 42.
2. Ibid., p. 90.
3. Ibid., p. 66.
4. Theocritus, "Idyl 3," *The Idyls of Theocritus, Bion, and Moschus*, trans. A. Lang (London, 1932), p. 20.
5. John Updike, *Assorted Prose* (New York, 1966), p. vii.
6. John Addington Symonds, *Studies of the Greek Poets* (New York, 1880), p. 240.
7. William Empson, *Some Versions of Pastoral* (London, 1950), p. 6.
8. Ibid., p. 12.
9. C. G. Jung, *Memories, Dreams, Reflections*, ed. Aniela Jaffe (New York, 1965), pp. 44, 171.
10. John F. Lynen, *The Pastoral Art of Robert Frost* (New Haven, 1960), p. 9.
11. Edith Hamilton, *Mythology* (New York, 1942), p. 22.
12. See F. W. W. Moorman, *Browne and Pastoral Poetry of the Elizabethan Age* (London, 1897); Hugh MacDonald, ed., *England's Helicon* (Harvard, 1950); Dorothy McCoy, *Tradition and Convention* (New York, 1965); and Andrew Young, *Poet and the Landscape* (London, 1962). The best work on the Renaissance pastoral tradition is Edward William Taylor's *Nature and Art in Renaissance Literature* (New York, 1964).
13. *Time*, "Books," April 26, 1968, p. 67.
14. Empson, pp. 3–23.
15. E. W. Taylor, *Art and Nature in the Renaissance* (New York, 1964), pp. 56–57. Taylor points out that this moral distinction did not overtly appear in the pastoral until Virgil's *Eclogues*. But because the moral assumption *did* pass into the

English language version of the pastoral, when it first entered the tradition seems a point of secondary significance.

16. See Emerson and Thoreau. For critical works see V. L. Parrington, *Main Currents in American Thought* (New York, 1927); Sherman Paul, *The Shores of America* (Urbana, Ill., 1958); F. O. Matthiesson, *American Renaissance* (New York, 1941, 1957); Richard Chase, *The American Novel and Its Tradition* (New York, 1957); Alfred Kazin, *On Native Grounds* (New York, 1942); Howard Mumford Jones, *The Frontier in American Fiction* (Jerusalem, Israel, 1956); Daniel G. Hoffman, *Form and Fable in American Fiction* (New York, 1961); Ihab Hassan, *Radical Innocence* (Princeton, 1961); Wilson O. Clough, *The Necessary Earth* (Austin, 1964); and Leo Marx, *The Machine in the Garden* (New York, 1964).

17. Empson, pp. 3–23.

18. Lynen, p. 140.

19. See C. G. Jung's *The Archetypes and the Collective Unconscious* (New York, 1934).

20. For a good discussion of this pattern in recent American novels, see David D. Galloway's *The Absurd Hero in American Fiction* (Austin, 1966), a treatment of the absurd man as saint, tragic hero, picaro, and seeker for love in the novels of John Updike, William Styron, Saul Bellow, and J. D. Salinger.

21. Empson, pp. 140–41.

22. Theocritus, "Idyl 10," p. 54.

23. Arthur Miller, *Death of a Salesman* (New York, 1967), p. 127.

2 – Versions of Pastoral and Anti-Pastoral Patterns in the American Tradition

1. John F. Lynen's *The Pastoral Art of Robert Frost* (New Haven, 1960), is of primary importance in understanding the American pastoral tradition, but he approaches the topic of the *anti*-pastoral rather obliquely. Other critics touch on the topic but do not pursue it in relation to its importance. See especially, Daniel G. Hoffman, *Form and Fable in American Fiction* (New York, 1961), pp. 47–49, and pp. 204–18; Ihab Hassan, *Radical Innocence* (Princeton, 1961), pp. 56, 102–5, 178; Richard Chase, *The American Novel and Its Tradition* (New York, 1957), p. 85 ff.; and Roy R. Male, *Hawthorne's Tragic Vision* (Austin, 1957), Chapter 8.

2. Thomas Morton, *The New English Canaan*, in *The Colonial Image*, ed. John C. Miller (New York, 1962), p. 76.

3. William Bradford, *History of Plymouth Plantation*, ed. Walter J. Black (New York, 1948), p. 85.

4. Ibid., p. 245.

5. Vernon L. Parrington, *Main Currents in American Thought*, Vol. 1 (New York, 1927), p. xi.

6. Edward William Taylor, *Art and Nature in the Renaissance* (New York, 1964), pp. 56–57.

7. Daniel G. Hoffman, *Form and Fable in American Fiction* (New York, 1961), p. 47. My italics.

8. Ibid., p. 49.

9. Ralph Waldo Emerson, *Nature*, included in *The Complete Works of Ralph Waldo Emerson* (Centenary Edition, New York, 1903–4), 1, p. 9.

10. John Updike, *Rabbit, Run* (New York, 1960), p. 8.

11. John Updike, *The Centaur* (New York, 1963), p. 291.

12. Compare Lang's translation of Theocritus' "Idyl 3," p. 20, and "Idyl 12," p. 64, for example. Both are love lyrics, the former heterosexual, and the latter homosexual.

13. Henry David Thoreau, *Walden* (Concord Edition, 20 vols., New York and Boston, 1906), 2, p. 355.

14. Henry David Thoreau, "Journal, 1843," *Selected Journals*, ed. Carl Bode (New York, 1967), p. 75.

15. For an excellent discussion of this story, see Daniel G. Hoffman's chapter, " 'The Maypole of Merry Mount' and the Folklore of Love," in *Form and Fable in American Fiction*, pp. 126–49.

16. Ibid., pp. 126–30.

17. Ibid., p. 129.

18. Ibid., p. 131.

19. Richard Chase, *The American Novel and Its Tradition* (New York, 1957), p. 85. See also, Roy R. Male, *Hawthorne's Tragic Vision* (Austin, 1957), p. 139.

20. Hoffman, p. 204.

21. Ibid., p. 215.

22. Quoted by Lionel Trilling in the "Introduction" to Mark Twain's *The Adventures of Huckleberry Finn* (New York, 1948), p. xv.

23. Ernest Hemingway, *The Sun Also Rises* (New York, 1926), pp. 108–22.

24. Ibid., p. 122.

25. F. Scott Fitzgerald, *The Great Gatsby* (New York, 1925), p. 29.

26. Ibid., p. 182.

27. Sinclair Lewis, *Babbitt* (New York, 1922), p. 6.

28. Ibid., p. 238.

29. Ibid., p. 239.

30. Ibid., p. 241.

31. Howard Mumford Jones, *The Frontier in American Fiction* (Jerusalem, Israel, 1956), p. 83.

32. In connection with Willa Cather's work, two books should be mentioned: *The Necessary Earth*, by Wilson O. Clough (Austin, 1964), and *The Middle Western Farm Novel in the Twentieth Century*, by Roy W. Meyer (Lincoln, Nebr., 1965). Both works deal somewhat with the same topic I have undertaken in this essay, and both works are valuable to the student of modern American literature. Neither, however, takes up the agrarian myth in terms of pastoral and anti-pastoral patterns. The Meyer book is especially valuable for an annotated, summarized list of "farm novels" in the appendix.

3—Primary Tensions: Eden and the Fall, Swain and Sophisticate, Farm and Town in Updike's Early Works

1. John Updike, "The Dogwood Tree: A Boyhood," *Assorted Prose* (New York, 1965), p. 180 ff.

2. John Updike, *The Poorhouse Fair* (New York, 1958), p. 107.

3. Ibid., p. 43.

4. John Updike, "Pigeon Feathers," *Pigeon Feathers and Other Stories* (New York, 1962), p. 118.

5. Ibid., p. 120.

6. Ibid., pp. 146–47.

7. Ibid., p. 149.

8. Ibid., pp. 149–50.

9. John Updike, "Foreword," *Olinger Stories: A Selection* (New York, 1964), p. viii.

10. Ibid., p. v.

11. Ibid., p. viii.

12. Ibid., p. v.

13. Updike, "The Dogwood Tree: A Boyhood," p. 159.

14. Ibid., pp. 160–61.

15. John Updike, *Couples* (New York, 1968), p. 148.

16. Updike, "Foreword," *Olinger Stories*, p. ix.

17. John Updike, "Friends from Philadelphia," *The Same Door* (New York, 1963), p. 3.

18. Updike, "Foreword," *Olinger Stories*, p. ix.

19. "Old and Precious" is found on p. 67 of Updike's

Assorted Prose; "Grandma Moses" is found on p. 101 in the same collection.

20. John Updike, "Old and Precious," *Assorted Prose* (New York, 1965), p. 70.

21. Ibid., pp. 69–70.

22. John Updike, "Grandma Moses," *Assorted Prose* (New York, 1965), p. 102.

23. Updike, *The Poorhouse Fair*, p. 27.

24. John Updike, *The Centaur* (New York, 1963), p. 268.

25. John Updike, "Packed Dirt, Churchgoing, A Dying Cat, A Traded Car," *Pigeon Feathers and Other Stories* (New York, 1962), p. 269.

26. Compare the strikingly similar descriptions in "Packed Dirt, Church-going, A Dying Cat, A Traded Car," pp. 269–70 and in *The Centaur*, pp. 266–67.

27. Quoted in Edward William Taylor's *Art and Nature in the Renaissance* (New York, 1964), p. 7.

4 – Rabbit, Run: *An Anti-Pastoral Satire*

1. "Kruppenbach," from German *Kruppe* (croup of a horse) and *Back* (backside). Kruppenbach, by the way, calls Rabbit a *Schussel*, p. 169, German (*coll.*) for a fidgety, hasty, or careless person. Compound German name-puns are a favorite trick of Updike's. For example, the neighboring farm in both *The Centaur* and *Of the Farm* is owned by "Schoelkopf," an auditory pun on the German *Scholl* (clod or sod) and *Kopf* (head): thus, "Clodhead."

2. See especially Howard M. Harper, Jr.'s "John Updike— The Intrinsic Problem of Human Existence," in *Desperate Faith* (Chapel Hill, 1967), p. 162 ff. Also see William Van O'Connor's "John Updike and William Styron: The Burdon of Talent," in *Contemporary American Novelists*, ed. Harry T. Moore (Carbondale, Ill., 1964), p. 205 ff. The last chapter of Ihab Hassan's *Radical Innocence* (Princeton, 1961), is a good general study of this type of hero.

3. The epigraph is from Pascal's *Pensee* 507.

4. John Updike, "Beerbohm and Others," *Assorted Prose* (New York, 1965), p. 255.

5. See Updike's *Verse: The Carpentered Hen and Telephone Poles* (New York, 1965), and his "Parodies" in *Assorted Prose* (New York, 1965), pp. 3–47.

6. Updike, "Beerbohm and Others," p. 255.

7. One of the best general studies of existential philosophy

is William Barrett's *Irrational Man* (New York, 1958), available in Anchor Books Edition, 1962.

8. John Updike, *Rabbit, Run* (New York, 1960), p. 132.

9. Ibid., p. 25.

10. Ibid., pp. 23–24.

11. Ibid., p. 15.

12. Ibid., p. 31.

13. Ibid., p. 36.

14. Ibid., p. 28.

15. Ibid., p. 86. My italics.

16. Ibid., p. 110.

17. Ibid., p. 113.

18. Ibid., p. 127.

19. Ibid., pp. 126–127.

20. Howard M. Harper, Jr., "John Updike—The Intrinsic Problem of Human Existence," *Desperate Faith* (Chapel Hill, 1967), p. 170.

21. Updike, *Rabbit, Run*, p. 137.

22. Ihab Hassan, *Radical Innocence* (Princeton, 1961), p. 325.

23. William Van O'Connor, "John Updike and William Styron: The Burden of Talent," *Contemporary American Novelists* (Carbondale, Ill., 1964), p. 211.

24. Roger D. Abrahams, "Androgynes Bound: Nathanael West's *Miss Lonelyhearts*," *Seven Contemporary Novelists*, ed. Thomas B. Whitbread (Austin, 1966), p. 55.

25. Abrahams, p. 54.

26. Gerry Brenner, "*Rabbit, Run*: John Updike's Criticism of the 'Return to Nature,'" *Twentieth Century Literature*, 12, No. 1 (April 1966), p. 14.

5—The Centaur: *Epic Paean and Pastoral Lament*

1. See A. Lang's "Introduction" to his translation of *The Idyls of Theocritus, Bion, and Moschus* (London, 1932), pp. xl–xli.

2. John Updike, *The Centaur* (New York, 1963), p. 97.

3. Ibid., pp. 93–94.

4. Theocritus, "Idyl 13," *The Idyls of Theocritus, Bion, and Moschus*, trans. A. Lang (London, 1932), p. 69.

5. Theocritus, "Idyl 22," p. 110.

6. Updike, *The Centaur*, p. 97.

7. Ibid., pp. 265–66.

8. Ibid., p. 267.

9. Ibid., p. 269.

10. Ibid., pp. 268–69.

11. Ibid., p. 171.

12. See Theocritus' "Idyl 4," for example.

13. Updike, *The Centaur*, pp. 296–97.

14. Ibid., p. 299. Translated by Steve Thornberry, University of Oklahoma. Incidentally, the Greek of the Fawcett Crest paperback edition is inaccurate, with two misspelled words. Use the Knopf edition.

15. Ibid., p. 61.

16. Ibid., p. 291.

17. Ibid., p. 59.

18. Ibid., pp. 61–62.

19. Ibid., p. 293.

20. Ibid., p. 74.

21. Ibid., p. 69.

22. Updike, "Foreword" to *Olinger Stories: A Selection* (New York, 1964), p. vi.

6 – The Wide-Hipped Wife and the Painted Landscape: Pastoral Ideals in Of the Farm

1. John Updike, *Of the Farm* (New York, 1965), p. 3.

2. William Barrett, *Irrational Man: A Study in Existential Philosophy* (New York, 1962), p. 102.

3. Updike, *Of the Farm*, p. 174.

4. Ibid., p. 4.

5. Ibid., p. 18.

6. Ibid., p. 31.

7. Ibid., p. 64.

8. Ibid., pp. 46–47.

9. Anthony Burgess, "Language, Myth, and Mr. Updike," *Commonweal*, 83 (February 1966), 559.

10. Updike, *Of the Farm*, pp. 58–59.

11. Ibid., p. 174.

7 – "Fields Still Steeped in Grace": Idyl and Irony in The Music School

1. John Updike, "In Football Season," *The Music School* (New York, 1966), p. 3.

2. Ibid., p. 4.

3. Theocritus, "Idyl 7," *The Idyls of Theocritus, Bion, and Moschus*, trans. A. Lang (London, 1932), p. 45.

4. Updike, "In Football Season," p. 7.

5. Ibid., p. 8.

6. Ibid., p. 8.

7. John Updike, "The Music School," *The Music School* (New York, 1966), p. 190.

8. Ibid., p. 190.

9. John Updike, "The Family Meadow," *The Music School* (New York, 1966), p. 232.

10. Ibid., p. 238.

11. John Updike, "The Hermit," *The Music School* (New York, 1966), p. 255.

12. Ibid., p. 256.

13. Ibid., p. 257.

14. Ibid., p. 259.

8—The Tarbox "Nymphs and Satyrs": Couples as a Didactic Anti-Pastoral

1. John Updike, quoted in *Time*, "Books," April 26, 1968, p. 67.

2. John Updike, *Couples* (New York, 1968), p. 106.

3. Ibid., p. 106.

4. Charles T. Samuels, "The Art of Fiction," (Updike interview) *Paris Review* (Winter 1968), p. 109.

5. For an example of this particular misreading of the novel, see Diana Trilling's "Updike's Yankee Traders," *Atlantic Monthly* (April 1968), p. 129.

6. Updike, *Couples*, p. 20.

7. Ibid., p. 17.

8. Ibid., p. 17.

9. Ibid., p. 52.

10. Ibid., p. 49.

11. Ibid., p. 54.

9—Moral Landscape in Bech: A Book

1. John Updike, *Bech: A Book* (New York, 1970), p. vi.

2. John Updike, "Foreword," *Olinger Stories: A Selection* (New York, 1964), p. vi.

3. John Updike, "Bech Enters Heaven," *Bech: A Book* (New York, 1970), p. 173.

4. John Updike, "The Bulgarian Poetess," *Bech: A Book* (New York, 1970), p. 62.

5. John Updike, "Bech Panics," *Bech: A Book* (New York, 1970), p. 125.

6. "A Gift from the City" is collected in John Updike's *The Same Door* (New York, 1959).

7. Updike, "The Bulgarian Poetess," p. 59.

8. Ibid., p. 62.

9. Updike, "Bech Panics," p. 125.

10. See John Updike's *Midpoint and Other Poems* (New York, 1969).

Selected Bibliography

Abrahams, Roger D. "Androgynes Bound: Nathanael West's *Miss Lonelyhearts*," *Seven Contemporary Novelists*, edited by Thomas B. Whitbread. Austin, 1966.

Barrett, William. *Irrational Man: A Study in Existential Philosophy*. New York, 1962.

Bradford, William. *History of Plymouth Plantation*. Edited by Walter J. Black. New York, 1948.

Brenner, Jerry. "*Rabbit, Run:* John Updike's Criticism of 'The Return to Nature,'" *Twentieth Century Literature*, 12 (April 1966), 3–14.

Burgess, Anthony. "Language, Myth, and Mr. Updike," *Commonweal*, 83 (February 1966), 557–59.

Chase, Richard. *The American Novel and Its Tradition*. New York, 1957.

Clough, Wilson O. *The Necessary Earth*. Austin, 1964.

Emerson, Ralph Waldo. *Nature*. Included in *The Complete Works of Ralph Waldo Emerson*, 1, Centenary Edition, New York, 1903–4.

Empson, William. *Some Versions of Pastoral*. London, 1935.

Fitzgerald, F. Scott. *The Great Gatsby*. New York, 1925.

Hamilton, Edith. *Mythology*. New York, 1942.

Hamilton, Kenneth and Alice. *John Updike: A Critical Essay*. Grand Rapids, 1969.

————. *Novel Perspective: The Elements of John Updike*. Grand Rapids, 1970.

Harper, Howard M., Jr. *Desperate Faith*. Chapel Hill, 1967.

Hassan Ihab. *Radical Innocence*. Princeton, 1961.

Hicks, Granville. "Generations of the Fifties: Malamud, Gold, and Updike." Essay in *The Creative Present*, edited by Nona Balakian and Charles Simmons. New York, 1963.

Hemingway, Ernest. *The Sun Also Rises*. New York, 1926.

Hoffman, Daniel G. *Form and Fable in American Fiction*. New York, 1961.

Jones, Howard Mumford. *The Frontier in American Fiction.* Jerusalem, Israel, 1956.

Jung, C. G. *Memories, Dreams, Reflections.* Edited by Aniela Jaffe. New York, 1965.

Kauffman, Stanley. "Onward with Updike," *New Republic* (September 24, 1966), 15–17.

Kazin, Alfred. *On Native Grounds.* New York, 1942.

Lang, A. Translator. *The Idyls of Theocritus, Bion, and Moschus.* London, 1932.

Lawrence, D. H. *Studies in Classic American Literature.* New York, 1930.

Lewis, C. S. *An Experiment in Criticism.* Cambridge, England, 1961.

Lynen, John F. *The Pastoral Art of Robert Frost.* New Haven, 1960.

Male, Roy R. *Hawthorne's Tragic Vision.* Austin, 1957.

Marx, Leo. *The Machine in the Garden.* New York, 1964.

Meyer, Roy W. *The Middlewestern Farm Novel in the Twentieth Century.* Lincoln, Nebr., 1965.

Miller, Arthur. *Death of a Salesman.* New York, 1967.

Miller, James E. *Quests Surd and Absurd.* Chicago, 1967.

Morton, Thomas. *The New English Canaan.* Included in *The Colonial Image,* edited by John C. Miller. New York, 1962.

O'Connor, William Van. "John Updike and William Styron: The Burden of Talent," *Contemporary American Novelists,* edited by Harry T. Moore. Carbondale, Ill., 1964.

Parrington, V. L. *Main Currents in American Thought,* 1. New York, 1927.

Samuels, Charles T. "A Place of Resonance," *Nation* (October 3, 1966), 328–29.

———. *John Updike.* Minneapolis, 1969.

———. "The Art of Fiction," (Updike interview), *Paris Review* (Winter 1968), 87–126.

Symonds, John Addington. *Studies of the Greek Poets.* New York, 1880.

Taylor, C. Clarke. *John Updike: A Bibliography.* Kent, Ohio, 1969.

Taylor, Edward William. *Nature and Art in Renaissance Literature.* New York, 1964.

Thoreau, Henry David. *Selected Journals of Henry David Thoreau.* Edited by Carl Bode. New York, 1967.

———. *Walden.* Concord Edition, 2. New York and Boston, 1906.

Time. Anonymous review and cover story, "Books" (April 26, 1968), 67–71.

Trilling, Diana. "Updike's Yankee Traders," *Atlantic Monthly* (April 1968), 129–31.

Trilling, Lionel. "Introduction," Mark Twain's *The Adventures of Huckleberry Finn.* New York, 1948.

Updike, John. *Assorted Prose.* New York, 1965.

––––––. *Bech: A Book.* New York, 1970.

––––––. *The Carpentered Hen and Other Tame Creatures.* New York, 1958.

––––––. *The Centaur.* New York, 1963.

––––––. *Couples.* New York, 1968.

––––––. "Eros Rampant," *Harper's Magazine* (June 1968), 59–64.

––––––. *Midpoint and Other Poems.* New York, 1969.

––––––. *The Music School.* New York, 1966.

––––––. *Of the Farm.* New York, 1965.

––––––. *Olinger Stories: A Selection.* New York, 1964.

––––––. *Pigeon Feathers and Other Stories.* New York, 1962.

––––––. *The Poorhouse Fair.* New York, 1959.

––––––. *Rabbit, Run.* New York, 1960.

––––––. *The Same Door.* New York, 1959.

––––––. *Telephone Poles and Other Poems.* New York, 1963.

––––––. "The Wait," *New Yorker* (February 17, 1968), 34–96.

West, Nathanael. *Miss Lonelyhearts.* Included in *The Complete Works of Nathanael West.* New York, 1966.

Index